PIZZA PILGRIMS

Pizza Pilgrims is the brainchild of James and Thom Elliot who decided to give up their 'proper' jobs to follow a dream. They travelled 2,500km around Italy in their Ape three-wheeler van, meeting food producers, top chefs and passionate local cooks along the way, to uncover the best-kept secrets of pizza making. Armed with their Italian foodie knowledge, they set up shop (or van) in Berwick Street market, Soho, selling incredible takeaway pizzas at a reasonable price. Since then they've fed hordes of hungry people on the street, at festivals and parties, as well as garnering five-star reviews for their food.

PIZZA PILGRIMS

Recipes from the Backstreets of Italy

JAMES AND THOM ELLIOT

HarperCollins*Publishers*

LIKE ALL GOOD IDEAS, IT STARTED IN THE PUB.

We had found ourselves with 'proper jobs' in London. Something had clearly gone wrong. We would meet up over a pint, discuss our predicament and devise harebrained schemes to get ourselves away from our desks and into something we really loved – food.

Having grown up in pubs run by our parents, we had been surrounded by food our whole lives. We had both dabbled in little projects which never amounted to much. James has the shortest Michelin-starred chef career of all time – seven hours at final count. Thom started a food blog – the first post is still pending.

But one summer's evening, when we had clearly had one pint too many, we hit on something that we both thought was a sure-fire winner. We had built up so much Dutch courage that we both agreed to hand in our notice the next day and make this plan happen. We were going to start a street food pizza company.

The street food scene had just exploded in London and encompassed everything we were looking for. It was driven by the passion of the people involved and was about choosing something you love and honing that skill until it's perfect. It also wasn't going to break the bank

and involved no angry chefs screaming in hot kitchens. We'd found our calling.

Two people acting on a whim is much more powerful (and dangerous) than one, and our little idea snowballed quickly. Within a week we had jumped on the idea of installing a pizza oven in a classic Italian Piaggio Ape van.

We told the world about our plan, only to be reassured by our friends that we were idiots. 'You have never made a pizza before in your lives.' 'No one has ever installed a 700kg stone oven in a tiny van like that.' Gleefully ignoring these concerns, we decided to crack on. We would fly to Italy, pick up the van and drive it 4,500km home. En route, we would visit all of Italy's top pizza destinations, picking up tips along the way. The Pizza Pilgrimage was born.

Before we knew it, we found ourselves behind the wheel of what was essentially a scooter with a van on the back. And thanks to the Ape's eye-watering top speed of 30mph, we were forced to keep off the motorway and stick to the path less trodden. This turned out to be the biggest blessing of the entire trip – it led us to discover so much more than the secrets of pizza.

'PIZZA IN ITALY IS LIKE A RELIGION'

As we all know, Italians are very proud of their food. Every Italian's mother is 'the best cook in the whole of Italy', which means that recipes and food concepts do not travel. You can taste something extraordinary in one small town, and they will denounce it as the devil's work just 10 miles away. Sticking to the back roads allowed us to discover things that we never would have found on the motorways.

Our little van's slower approach to life (we were even overtaken by a jogger going up a hill) also meant that we were able to see how the country's geography influences the food. In the South, the food is based around 'cucina povera' – or 'poverty food' – borne out of necessity and lack of money. Meat is expensive and, as such, rare. Dishes focus on the fruits and vegetables that they have in abundance, bulked up with breads, pastas and rice.

As you head north, past the bright lights of Rome and towards 'swanky' cities like Milan, the weather gets colder and the food gets richer. Expensive delicacies such as Parma ham, Parmesan cheese and truffles begin to feature more prominently in what is essentially rich food for rich people.

Back in London we wrestled the oven into the back of our van and set up shop on Berwick Street, an old fruit and veg market in the heart of Soho. We really like how our new home has so many parallels with Naples – it's loud and dirty with great food and amazing characters. Everyone knows each other and everyone's open to a deal. And with pizza as a currency, we haven't paid for a coffee or a haircut since we started! It has been a brilliant, fun, exciting, nerve-racking year. Even the old boys who have been trading on the market for decades are on board with our little pizza van now – they have finally stopped calling us 'The Apprentice'.

This book captures everything we have learned, so you can make great pizzas and other lesser known Italian classics at home. It's a collection of our own creations and recipes straight from the Italian horse's mouth, so to speak. Just like Mamma used to make.

Enjoy!

🌐 www.pizzapilgrims.co.uk
🐦 @pizzapilgrims

🌐 For an interactive map go to www.pizzapilgrims.co.uk

HOME

9 – **Genoa** – We met Paolo the basil farmer and found out his amazing pesto recipe.

8 – **Reggio Emilia** – A visit to a Parmesan factory to see one of Italy's greatest exports being made.

5 – **Caserta** – Where we milked a buffalo and learned how mozzarella di bufala Campana is produced.

4 – **Naples** – The big one – the spiritual home of pizza. Highlights included a tour of Caputo flour mill, the best Margherita we have ever tasted at Da Michele pizzeria, pizza fritta in the Spanish quarter and rum baba.

7 – **Pisa** – We met Giuseppe, an olive farmer who showed us around his farm, followed by a visit to the local olive press to watch his olives being made into oil.

8 – *Reggio Emilia*

7 – *Pisa*

9 – *Genoa*

6 - *Rome*

5 - *Caserta*

4 - *Naples*

3 - *Sarno*

2 - *Spilinga*

1 - *Reggio Di Calabria*

6 - Rome – We met Gabriele Bonci who was whipping up a pizza al taglio storm at The Pizzarium.

3 - Sarno – Where we discovered the secrets of San Marzano tomatoes and met Antonino Esposito – our pizza guru.

2 - Spilinga – The home of nduja spicy sausage – one of our favourite discoveries from the trip.

1 - Reggio Di Calabria – Where we picked up 'Concetta' – our little Piaggio Ape van.

THE PIZZA PILGRIMAGE

A map to show you the route we took, the regions of Italy we travelled through and the key stops you need to make a Neapolitan pizza...

STREET FOOD AND SNACKS

We couldn't resist starting off with some street food. Everyone is raving about London's street food scene at the moment, but the truth is that Rome and Naples have been flying the street food flag for centuries. There are so many delicious, portable creations that it is hard to see why anyone bothers to eat inside (that is, until you try the pizzerias). We have rounded up a selection of our favourites here for you to try at home, but please don't feel compelled to head out onto the street to eat them. They taste just as good indoors.

———

Supplì al telefono are the lesser known siblings of arancini – a Roman version of the Sicilian classic and a staple on the streets of Italy's capital. They get their name from their mozzarella centre, which stretches out like a telephone wire when they're broken in half (just like a Pizza Hut ad). Next time you make a ragù (see our recipe on page 134), make too much and freeze it. It's a great thing to have in the freezer anyway and means you can make these supplì really easily.

Supplì al telefono
(risotto balls filled with mozzarella)

MAKES 15–20 SUPPLÌ

LAZIO

Glug of olive oil
60g butter
350g risotto rice
1 litre beef or chicken stock (stock cube is fine)
500g ragù (from your favourite recipe or use the leftovers from our Neapolitan Ragù Sunday Dinner on page 134)
100g Parmesan, grated
Sea salt
1 ball of mozzarella, cut into 1.5cm cubes
Plain flour, for dusting
2 eggs, beaten
Breadcrumbs, for coating
Vegetable oil, for deep-frying

Put a large saucepan on a medium heat and add a glug of olive oil with half the butter.

When the butter starts to foam, add the rice and toast for 2 minutes until the grains start to go translucent.

Add enough stock to just cover the rice and gently simmer. Keep topping up with stock for roughly 30 minutes until it has reduced to a risotto-like consistency and the rice is al dente (still with a little resistance when you bite into a grain).

Add your ragù, the rest of the butter, Parmesan and sea salt and stir until the cheese has melted and it has taken on a glossy sheen.

Spread the risotto out on a large plate and leave to cool.

To make the rice balls, take a small piece of the mixture, definitely no bigger than a golf ball. Roll into a ball and then flatten in your palm to a thickness of about 1cm. Take a cube of the mozzarella and place in the middle of the disc.

Wrap the rice around the mozzarella using the palm of your hand so that the cheese is completely encased in the rice. Put a little water on your hands and roll the ball into the classic oval shape. Repeat until you've used up all the mixture.

Roll the balls in flour, followed by the beaten egg, then the breadcrumbs. To get a really good crust, repeat the egg and breadcrumbs steps.

Heat the oil to 180°C (if a cube of bread browns in 15–20 seconds, the oil is hot enough). Taking care with the hot oil, deep-fry the balls for 3–4 minutes until golden brown and the mozzarella is melted and stringy when you break one open. If you cook them too fast, then they brown too quickly and the mozzarella doesn't melt.

Directly translating as 'mixed fry', fritto misto is just taking anything you love and frying it in a light batter. It is traditionally a seaside dish, with seafood featuring heavily, but on our trip we saw everything from fried courgettes to potato croquettes. It's up to you.

Fritto misto with lemon mayonnaise

SERVES 4–6

CAMPANIA

Ingredients to take your pick from…

Whitebait

Small whole shrimps (you eat the head and all…)

Shelled tiger prawns

Squid rings and tentacles

Courgette chips (cut your courgettes into batons)

Trimmed artichoke hearts

Whole sage leaves

Cavolo nero leaves

…or anything else that you fancy frying

For the batter

75g plain flour (seasoned with sea salt and black pepper)

1 litre milk

Groundnut or vegetable oil, for deep-frying

1 lemon

For the lemon mayonnaise

2 egg yolks

200ml groundnut or sunflower oil

50ml extra virgin olive oil

Grated zest and juice of a ½ lemon

Pinch of sea salt

First, make the lemon mayonnaise. Whisk the 2 egg yolks in a small mixing bowl. Slowly trickle in the oils while constantly whisking until you have a thick emulsion. Then, whisk in the lemon zest and the juice and season to taste with sea salt. This mayonnaise will keep in an airtight container for a good couple of weeks.

Take two trays and put the seasoned flour in one and the milk in the other.

Then, keeping one 'dry' hand and one 'wet' hand (to prevent ending up with a completely battered hand!), throw your chosen fish and vegetables into the flour, followed by the milk, and then back in the flour again. This should build up a good coating of flour, but not a thick fish-and-chips style batter.

Heat 10cm of the oil in a heavy-bottom saucepan. You know the oil is hot enough when a 2–3cm cube of white bread browns in 30 seconds.

Taking care with the hot oil, simply deep-fry everything, making sure not to overcrowd the pan and turning everything until they are crispy with a light golden brown colour.

Drain on kitchen paper, season with salt and lemon juice and eat with the lemon mayonnaise.

Calabrians are a committed bunch and are even extremely proud of their onions! In the seaside town of Tropea, every tourist shop sells buckets, spades and massive bunches of onions. They are so popular that Tonino, self-proclaimed 'ice cream genius', even makes red onion gelato. Tropean or not, this recipe is all about good onions. It lasts for a couple of weeks in the fridge and should go with most Italian cheeses, though it's hard to beat on a good English Cheddar toastie. In fact, we are still searching for something that it does not go with.

TROPEAN RED ONION JAM

MAKES 1 LARGE JAR

CALABRIA

4 large red onions
2 tablespoons olive oil
Sea salt and black pepper
150ml (a small glass) of
  red wine
60ml balsamic vinegar
1 tablespoon light
  muscovado sugar (though
  caster sugar will do)

Peel the onions, halve them through the root and slice lengthways.

In a heavy-bottom saucepan, heat the olive oil and add the onion with a pinch of salt. Put a lid on and cook over a low heat for about 15 minutes until the onion is soft and translucent.

Add the red wine, balsamic vinegar, sugar and pepper and reduce down for about 15 minutes over a low heat with the lid on, then for another 10 minutes over a medium heat with the lid off until you have a sticky 'jam' consistency.

The jam will keep in an airtight sterilized jar (just immerse the jar in boiling water) in the fridge for up to 2 weeks.

TONINO

ONION JAM

To a Londoner, chestnuts are a bit of a novelty. Come Christmas, the old oil drums are wheeled out and the chestnuts are ceremoniously burned to a dry crisp over hot coals. In Tuscany, however, chestnuts have a much firmer fixture and are part of the staple diet of the region. They're hugely versatile and can be used in sweet and savoury dishes – from whole chestnuts in soups to chestnut flour in cakes. Here's two of our favourite ways to use them.

ROAST CHESTNUTS ON THE BBQ
TUSCANY

The truth is, Nat King Cole was a rubbish cook. He did, however, have this recipe right. 'Chestnuts roasting on an open fire' are delicious. As the shells char, the flesh becomes smoky and sweet. Simply cut a small cross in the base of each chestnut to stop them exploding and then throw them on the BBQ.

This is our version of the classic Tuscan chestnut purée. We've added dark chocolate in homage to a certain Italian brand of hazelnut and chocolate spread, which some people with a more 'sophisticated' palate turn their noses up at. We, on the other hand, have been known to eat it straight out of the jar with a spoon!

ROAST CHESTNUT AND DARK CHOCOLATE SPREAD

MAKES ABOUT 4 JAM JARS WORTH

TUSCANY

1kg chestnuts
400g caster sugar
200g dark chocolate
   (70% cocoa content),
   broken up into pieces
Pinch of sea salt

To get the best flavour from the chestnuts, roast them in the oven for 15 minutes at 250°C/230°C fan/Gas 9 or BBQ them using the technique we've just mentioned.

Once roasted, peel the shells and rub them in a tea towel until the papery underskin comes off.

Place the peeled chestnuts in a pan and add water until just covered. Add the sugar and boil for about 10 minutes until the chestnuts are tender.

Drain the chestnuts, reserving the cooking water, and blitz them in a food processor with 200ml of the cooking water until you have a smooth paste.

Return the mixture to the saucepan and boil for around 10 minutes until it has achieved a 'jammy' consistency.

Take off the heat and stir in the broken up chocolate.

Add a small pinch of salt.

Sterilize some airtight jars by immersing them in boiling water. Allow the spread to cool and store in the sterilized jars. It should keep in the fridge for 1 week.

The spread is great in cakes and puddings, but is best eaten on toasted sourdough bread.

Porcini literally means 'piglet' in Italian, which makes sense as these mushrooms are fat and have a meaty texture. This has led to them being dubbed the 'king of the mushrooms'. Fresh porcini are highly prized all over Italy, but it's much easier to get hold of the dried versions and we actually think they work better in this recipe. These breaded porcini are great served with steak. Or just eat them straight out of the pan.

BREADED PORCINI WITH THYME SALT

SERVES 4

TUSCANY

400ml chicken stock
2 tablespoons balsamic vinegar
1 teaspoon caster sugar
16 large slices of dried porcini mushroom
100g plain flour (seasoned with sea salt and black pepper)
3 eggs, beaten
3 good handfuls of breadcrumbs
Groundnut or vegetable oil, for deep-frying
1 teaspoon sea salt
Black pepper
Sprig of thyme
1 lemon

First you need to soak the mushrooms to reconstitute them. Heat the chicken stock and add the balsamic vinegar and sugar.

Take the stock off the heat and add in the mushrooms. Leave to steep for 20–30 minutes.

Once the mushrooms have softened and grown in size, drain from the stock (do not throw away the stock as it can be used for the base of a stew, soup or risotto etc.).

Roll the mushrooms in the flour, then the egg and then the breadcrumbs, before repeating the egg and breadcrumbs steps to ensure a good thick crust.

Heat the oil to 180°C (if a cube of bread browns in 15–20 seconds, the oil is hot enough). Taking care with the hot oil, deep-fry the mushrooms for about 3 minutes until the crust is golden brown and the mushrooms have softened.

In a pestle and mortar, grind together the salt with a good pinch of pepper and the leaves from a sprig of thyme.

Serve the breaded porcini with lemon wedges and a scattering of the thyme salt mix.

We ate our body weight in these polenta chips at a Tuscan village donkey race, as you do… They can be eaten with pretty much anything, from grilled fish to stews. To be honest, we like them on their own with beer and lots of salt.

DEEP-FRIED POLENTA CHIPS WITH ROSEMARY SALT

TUSCANY

MAKES 20—25 CHIPS

250g quick-cook polenta, plus 50g for dusting
Large handful of grated Parmesan
50g butter
Sea salt and black pepper
Vegetable oil, for deep-frying
Sprig of rosemary

Cook the polenta according to the packet instructions.

Once cooked, take off the heat and stir in the Parmesan, butter and a good pinch of salt and pepper.

Spread the mixture out on a greased tray, 2–3cm thick, and leave to cool/set.

Cut or tear the polenta into mouth-sized strips and roll in the uncooked polenta (this will add a good crunch when cooked).

Heat the oil to 180°C (if a cube of bread browns in 15–20 seconds, the oil is hot enough). Taking care with the hot oil, deep-fry the chips for about 4 minutes until golden brown.

Take the leaves off a sprig of rosemary and crush with sea salt in a pestle and mortar. Either sprinkle this over the chips or put in a bowl to the side for dipping.

Hidden away in the backstreets of Venice, you'll find little bars called 'bacaros'. These are where the locals go to escape the hoards of tourists, drink good wine and snack on cicchetti – essentially Italian tapas. Polpette are little meatballs, served in a simple tomato sauce, and they are definitely the stars of the show, for us anyway.

VENETIAN POLPETTE WITH TOMATO SAUCE

SERVES 4

VENETO

2 slices of stale white bread
100ml milk
300g minced beef
200g minced pork
1 large egg
Small handful of grated
   Parmesan
Sea salt and black pepper
1 small onion, finely diced
2 cloves of garlic, minced
2 tablespoons olive oil
3 tins of San Marzano (or
   any good-quality Italian)
   tomatoes, chopped
Large handful of basil leaves
Olive oil

Break up the stale bread into a large mixing bowl and cover with the milk. Allow the bread to absorb all of the milk and leave for about 10 minutes until just softened.

Add the beef, pork, egg, Parmesan and a pinch of salt and pepper. Combine everything together.

Allow the mixture to rest in the fridge for about 20 minutes.

In a large saucepan, gently fry the onion and garlic in the olive oil.

Pour in the tomatoes and 100ml water, bring to the boil and simmer for 10 minutes to cook the tomatoes. Check for seasoning.

Take the meat mixture from the fridge and roll it into golf-ball-sized meatballs.

Poach the meatballs in the sauce for about 10 minutes until they are cooked through.

Take off the heat and stir through the basil leaves. Serve with grated Parmesan and olive oil.

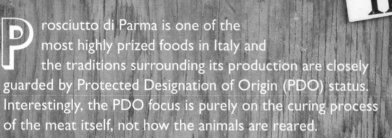

PARMA HAM

Prosciutto di Parma is one of the most highly prized foods in Italy and the traditions surrounding its production are closely guarded by Protected Designation of Origin (PDO) status. Interestingly, the PDO focus is purely on the curing process of the meat itself, not how the animals are reared.

It takes 4 months just to prep the pork legs for the curing process – a combination of massaging, salt baths, chilling, hot showers (essentially a recreation of Joan Collins's daily routine). Once this is complete, the curing process begins. The ham is not worthy to go by the name of prosciutto di Parma before it has been hung for at least another 4 months. All in all, it almost takes as long to make a Parma ham as it does to make a baby! The best and most sought-after hams are cured for over 3 years!

In order to test that the ham is up to the required standard, one man must test each ham using years of detailed knowledge and, unexpectedly, a small, sharpened horse bone. However, if you want to test the quality of a Parma ham yourself, you can do so without this essential tool. If it has been properly cured, the fat on the ham should easily melt away between your fingers. Tastewise, you are looking for a good balance of salt and sweet, but without any trace of the flavour of pork.

A variation of the Mozzarella in Carozza (see recipe on page 36), these are made from fried slices of aubergine and smoked scamorza. This cheese is similar to a mozzarella, but has been lightly smoked for a deeper flavour, making it one for the more discerning palate...

MELANZANE IN CAROZZA WITH SCAMORZA
(AUBERGINE SANDWICHES WITH SOFT CHEESE)

MAKES 6 SANDWICHES

CAMPANIA

2 aubergines
Sea salt and black pepper
6 slices of smoked scamorza
1 small bunch of sage leaves
Plain flour, for coating
3 eggs, beaten
3 large handfuls of
   breadcrumbs
Olive oil, for shallow-frying

Cut 12 good slices of aubergine, about 1cm thick.

Salt the sliced aubergine and leave to drain in a colander for at least an hour.

Next, rinse and dry the slices. This process helps to extract some of the bitterness from the aubergine and allows for more flavour to be absorbed.

Sandwich a slice of scamorza and a sage leaf between two slices of the aubergine.

Dredge the sandwich in flour, then in the beaten egg, followed by the breadcrumbs.

Shallow-fry in olive oil (nothing too expensive) until golden brown.

Once you have shallow-fried all six sandwiches, throw a handful of sage leaves into the oil and fry for about 10 seconds until they stop spitting and have gone crisp.

Serve on a plate, sprinkled with sea salt and scattered with sage leaves.

Artichokes are everywhere in Italy, and each region has their own favourite way to cook them. In Palermo you get a whole, boiled artichoke in a paper cone with fresh salsa to eat right away, while in Rome marinated artichoke hearts are a refined antipasti dish. This is our favourite, served whole with a delicious warm anchovy and garlic dip called 'bagna cauda', Italian for 'hot bath'.

WHOLE GLOBE ARTICHOKE WITH BAGNA CAUDA (ANCHOVY DIP)

SERVES 4
(OR 2 HUNGRY ARTICHOKE LOVERS!)

PIEDEMONT

1 whole globe artichoke
12 cloves of garlic
Milk, to cover
10 anchovy fillets
100g unsalted butter
150ml extra virgin olive oil
Juice of a ¼ lemon
Sea salt and black pepper

Trim off the bottom of the artichoke stem, leaving just a few centimetres on.

Rinse under cold water and then boil in salted water for 25–40 minutes or until the outer leaves pull away easily.

To make the bagna cauda, peel the garlic cloves, place in a small saucepan and cover with milk.

Simmer on a low heat for about 10 minutes until the garlic cloves have gone tender and sweet.

Using a food processor or a stick blender, blitz the milk and the garlic together until smooth.

Next, add in the anchovy fillets, butter, olive oil and lemon juice and blitz again until smooth. Check for seasoning – the sauce should pack a punch, but not be acrid, and the sweetness of the garlic and milk should come through.

To eat, pull the leaves off the artichoke, dip in the warm sauce and scrape the flesh off with your teeth. It's not pretty, but it's damn tasty!

When you get down to the heart, scrape out the furry centre (the 'choke') with a teaspoon. The heart can then be cut into wedges and eaten as well.

You'd be forgiven for not jumping at the opportunity to make this at first glance. Whipped, reconstituted salt cod... Mmmmm! But this Venetian snack is another great example of the Italian mentality to make the best of what you've got. A great, and cheap, place to get salt cod in the UK is a Caribbean supermarket where they have it stacked up in huge piles. You can also find it at your local fishmonger, who will have it presoaked and ready to cook.

BACCALÀ MANTECATO
(SALT COD PÂTÉ)
VENETO

SERVES 4

300g presoaked salt cod (or 150g unsoaked)
150ml milk
Sea salt
50ml flavourless oil (such as groundnut or sunflower oil)
50ml olive oil (not extra virgin as the flavour will overpower the fish)
1 small clove of garlic
Small handful of parsley, chopped
Squeeze of lemon juice
Bread or polenta, to serve

If using unsoaked salt cod, soak in cold water for 12 hours or more (depending on the thickness), changing the water at least three times. Once it has doubled in weight and is firm but tender, it's ready to use.

Place the fish in a saucepan and (just) cover with water, then add the milk. Add a good pinch of salt, which seems a little strange when you've just spent all that time getting the salt out, but this way you're in control of how salty it is.

Bring to the boil and poach the fish for about 5 minutes. Skim off any foam that rises to the top as the fish cooks.

Drain the fish and transfer to a mixing bowl. Start to break down the fish using a wooden spoon and begin to drizzle in the oils in a steady stream. Keep whipping until you have used all the oil and you have a thick and roughly textured pâté.

Crush the garlic clove with salt under the back of a knife until you have a paste. Add to the pâté with the parsley and a squeeze of lemon.

If the pâté is too thick, let it out with a little milk.

This is great served on bruschetta or you can eat it like the Venetians on grilled polenta slices (see the recipe on page 150 for making polenta. To make polenta slices, spread the polenta into a 2–3cm deep tray and set in the fridge for 1–2 hours before turning out, slicing and grilling).

Italian's love porchetta. Wherever there's a festival or national holiday in Italy, the trusty porchetta vendors will be there in their little vans dishing out pork sandwiches with salsa verde. It's such a national obsession you can even get a great porchetta panini at service stations up and down the Autostrada – don't expect that on the M1! This recipe will serve ten to twelve people, but even if it's dinner for one, always make this much. Porchetta is the king of leftovers!

Porchetta

ACROSS ITALY

1 whole deboned and butterflied pork belly (get your butcher to do this), approx. 5kg
Grated zest and juice of 1 lemon
Sea salt and black pepper
6 cloves of garlic, chopped
Bunch of chopped parsley
Handful of sage leaves
1 sprig of rosemary, leaves picked
2 sprigs of thyme, leaves picked
Large handful of pine nuts
2 teaspoons fennel seeds
Olive oil
Ciabatta, to serve

For the gravy
1 onion, roughly chopped
2 carrots, roughly chopped
2 celery stalks, roughly chopped
1 whole head of garlic
1 glass of white wine

First, preheat your oven as high as it will go.

Take your pork belly and lay it out flat, with the skin facing down. Slash the flesh of the belly with a sharp knife in a crisscross fashion, about 1cm deep. This will increase the surface area and allow for more flavour.

Combine the lemon juice and zest and rub into the meat before seasoning generously with salt and pepper.

Take the garlic, herbs, pine nuts and fennel seeds and scatter evenly over the pork belly, again ensuring that you work the flavours into the flesh. Drizzle with olive oil.

Now, roll the belly as tightly as you can before tying with butcher's string. There are some very clever 'cheffy' ways of doing this, but we reckon as long as it's tight and it holds, then it's all good!

Rub the skin with a little olive oil and season again with salt.

Place in a deep roasting tin on a bed of the onion, carrot, celery and garlic. This will stop the porchetta from frying on the bottom and the vegetables will help make an amazing gravy.

Roast in the hot oven for 10 minutes before turning the oven down to 160°C/140°C fan/Gas 3 and cooking for 2–3 hours until the skin has become crackling and the meat is tender and pulls away.

To make the gravy, put the roasting tin on the hob and deglaze with the glass of white wine and a glass of water. Use a wooden spoon to scrape all the caramelized meat and veg off the bottom of the pan and then reduce to an intense gravy.

We think the best way to eat this is on a freshly baked ciabatta with our Salsa Verde (see recipe on page 34), a spoon of the gravy and a few beers...

You've got to love salsa verde! It's a great thing to keep in the fridge and finds its way into everything from roasts to sandwiches. It's essentially an olive oil and lemon dressing packed with handfuls of punchy flavours. When done properly, it should be a perfect balance of sweet, sour, salt and savoury – and moreish like you wouldn't believe.

Salsa Verde

ACROSS ITALY

MAKES 1 JAR

Large handful of parsley
Large handful of basil
1 tablespoon capers
5 anchovy fillets
Handful of pitted green olives
1 small clove of garlic
Sea salt and black pepper
Olive oil
Juice of 1 lemon

Finely chop the parsley, basil, capers, anchovies and olives into a bowl.

Crush the clove of garlic with salt using the back of your knife and add to the bowl.

Add olive oil to loosen. The mixture should have a dropping consistency (a bit like risotto).

Then add the lemon juice, and salt and pepper to taste. Spoon into an airtight sterilized jar (just immerse the jar in boiling water) and cover with 1cm olive oil. The salsa will keep in the fridge for up to 2 weeks.

Translated as 'mozzarella in a carriage', this is the Italian version of a cheese toastie, albeit more refined. Buffalo mozzarella and anchovies put plastic ham and processed cheese to shame. You can't really go wrong here.

MOZZARELLA IN CAROZZA

CAMPANIA

MAKES 4 SANDWICHES

2 x 125g balls of buffalo
  mozzarella, sliced
4 anchovy fillets
8 slices of normal white
  bread (crusts off)
Sea salt and black pepper
3 eggs, beaten
Olive oil, for shallow-frying

Sandwich a slice of mozzarella and an anchovy fillet between two slices of bread.

Then, turn the sandwich over in the seasoned beaten egg until completely covered.

Shallow-fry in olive oil until golden brown and the mozzarella is melted.

Serve, eat and most likely repeat...

STARTERS

Anyone who has been invited for dinner at an Italian home knows that the word 'starter' has never been more aptly used. Italian generosity really knows no bounds when it comes to food, so many of the meals that we enjoyed on our trip became real tests of stamina (who needs marathons!). Italian starters are also a brilliant opportunity for Italians to show off their national obsession with quality and simplicity – and the following are some of our favourites from our trip.

———

We met up with some students who had been in touch on Twitter and wanted to take us to their favourite pizza place in Rome. It was called F1, a brilliant no-frills pizzeria, but we remember it as the first place we tasted true Roman fiori di zucca. Deep-fried in a really light batter, it is important to eat them as quickly as you can – not least to stop everyone else beating you to it! Courgette flowers can be hard to track down in the UK, but they can be ordered from good greengrocers or online.

FIORI DI ZUCCA FRITTI ALLA ROMANA
(DEEP-FRIED STUFFED COURGETTE FLOWERS)

MAKES 10 STUFFED
COURGETTES

LAZIO

180g plain flour
20g cornflour
10 courgette flowers
2 x 125g balls of buffalo
  mozzarella (cow's milk
  mozzarella will also do)
10 anchovy fillets
Groundnut or other
  flavourless oil, for
  deep-frying

For the batter, mix the flour and cornflour with 200ml ice cold water. Unlike most batters, you don't want it to be too smooth and little pockets of flour are good as they will go really crispy.

Take each courgette flower and trim away any excess stem. Then stuff each flower with a slice of mozzarella and an anchovy.

Gently dip into the batter, holding onto the stem. Heat the oil to 180°C (if a cube of bread browns in 15–20 seconds, the oil is hot enough). Taking care of the hot oil, deep-fry the courgette flowers in batches for 2–3 minutes until crisp and a light golden brown. Remove from the oil, drain on kitchen paper and serve.

Frittata is a dish that often gets mistreated in Italy. Visions of grey, sponge-like cakes sitting for days in service station display cabinets still send shudders down our spines. However, a lovingly made frittata with fresh eggs and great ingredients can be one of the finest foods the country has to offer. Always look at what you have to hand and think seasonally. This recipe is a really summery example and a great use of leftover spaghetti.

PRAWN, PEA AND SPAGHETTI FRITTATA

CAMPANIA

SERVES 2 HUNGRY
OR 4 NORMAL PEOPLE

4 large eggs, lightly beaten
2 spring onions, finely chopped
Small handful of parsley, chopped
A pinch of peperoncino (dried chilli flakes)
Sea salt and black pepper
100g uncooked king prawns
Olive oil
150g cooked spaghetti
2 handfuls of frozen peas

In a bowl, mix together the eggs, spring onion, parsley and the chilli flakes. Season with salt and pepper.

Get a medium-sized frying pan with a lid on a high heat and quickly fry the prawns in 2 tablespoons of olive oil. The idea here is to put some colour on the prawns, but not completely cook them as they will carry on cooking in the eggs.

Next add the cooked spaghetti to the pan and spread evenly before scattering over the frozen peas.

Pour over the egg mixture, cover and cook on a medium heat for 5 minutes.

Once the bottom has taken on a golden brown colour it's time to flip the frittata (fingers crossed!). Place a plate over the frying pan and, in one big move, flip the pan and the plate 180 degrees. Then, with the pan back on the heat, slide the frittata back into the pan, cooked side up.

Cook for a further 2–3 minutes with the lid off.

You can eat this straight away with a fresh green salad or cold as part of a picnic or antipasti board.

In the south of Italy, chilli is a way of life and they are not shy of adding it to *everything* they eat. We spent an entire day at a farm outside Sapri in Campania tasting chilli varieties and products – everything from chocolate and chilli liquor to chilli sweets.

Peperoncino, as it is known locally, comes in two main varieties – sweet and hot. They are measured for spiciness using the Scoville scale, ranging from a score of one for a normal bell pepper to two million for pepper spray!

One of the most popular varieties in Italy are 'perco sacko' chillies, so called because their pointy shape causes them to poke through the bags that they are transported in. However, the highlight of the day was convincing Thom to try a Naga chilli. Even an hour drinking yoghurt didn't help the heat subside.

Drying chillies is a great way to preserve them. They will keep for months or years and they develop a warm, smoky flavour that you don't get from fresh chillies. Also, when they are hung up in the kitchen, they look fantastic!

DRYING CHILLIES IS REALLY EASY:

1. Get hold of a box of red chillies (from your local fruit and veg market), a heavy-duty needle and some thread.

2. Cut a piece of thread and tie a knot in one end. Put the other end of the thread through the eye of the needle.

3. Push the needle through the green stem of the chilli, pushing the chilli to the end of the string.

4. Keep adding chillies until you have a full string with chillies pointing in every direction. Make sure the chillies are evenly distributed when you hang the string, and that they are not bunched up on one side.

5. Keep going! The world record for a 'ristra', as these strings are called, is 113 metres.

6. Hang your ristra in a warm dry place, making sure air can get to every chilli.

This is hardly even a recipe, more a collection of great ingredients which go brilliantly together. It's the perfect example of the Italian mentality of keeping things simple. Asparagus season in the UK is a mere eight weeks, starting in early May, so make sure you don't miss out. And keep a close eye on the butter – there is a really fine line between browned butter and burnt butter.

ASPARAGUS ALLA MILANESE
(ASPARAGUS WITH FRIED EGG, PARMESAN AND BROWNED BUTTER)

SERVES 4

LOMBARDY

Large bunch of asparagus
  (about 20 spears)
80g butter
4 large free-range eggs
Squeeze of lemon juice
Handful of grated Parmesan

Holding each asparagus spear at both ends, bend until it naturally snaps at the point where the spear is woody. Discard this woody bit.

Cook the spears in salted boiling water for about 3–4 minutes until tender, but still with a bite. Separate the spears among your four serving plates.

In a frying pan, heat the butter until foaming, then add in your eggs, ensuring the yolks remain intact.

Gently fry for 2–3 minutes until the whites have set but the yolks are still runny.

Using a spatula, take the eggs from the pan and lay on top of the asparagus spears.

If it hasn't taken colour already, turn up the heat and cook the butter until lightly browned. Take off the heat and add a small squeeze of lemon juice.

Finally pour the butter over the asparagus and eggs before coating generously with the grated Parmesan.

Panzanella is a great way to use up stale bread – the crustier the better. This salad is pretty versatile and can be made with anything you can get your hands on really. Feel free to experiment and come up with your own combinations!

Panzanella

TUSCANY

1 small and stale white loaf, a couple of days old, cut into chunks

4 vine-ripened tomatoes, roughly chopped

½ a cucumber, roughly chopped

1 red onion, finely sliced into half moons

2 tablespoons capers, drained

Sea salt and black pepper

5 tablespoons olive oil

3 tablespoons red wine vinegar

Large pinch of caster sugar

Large handful of basil leaves

In a large mixing bowl, combine the bread, tomato, cucumber, onion and capers. Season with salt and pepper.

In a separate bowl, mix together the olive oil, vinegar and sugar until it has emulsified and the sugar has dissolved.

Add the dressing to the salad with the basil and toss everything together.

Leave the salad to macerate, or soften, for at least an hour before eating. Overnight in the fridge is even better as it will give it time for all the flavours to marry together and mellow.

Why more people don't make their own gnocchi is beyond us. It's quick, cheap and the only tool you need is a fork! They can be served with a really simple sage butter sauce (see our recipe on page 166) or with any sauce you love with pasta. One of our favourites is on the next page.

Making gnocchi

TUSCANY

SERVES 4

450g full-fat ricotta cheese (this can be substituted for 450g mashed potato for traditional gnocchi)
1 large egg
Small handful of grated Parmesan
180g plain flour
Sea salt and black pepper

To make the gnocchi, put the ricotta in a colander over a bowl and leave in the fridge for about an hour to drain off any excess moisture.

In a mixing bowl, beat together the drained ricotta, egg, Parmesan, flour and season to taste with salt and pepper.

Once combined, turn the mixture out onto a lightly floured surface and knead it until you have a smooth and soft dough.

Cut your dough ball into six pieces and roll each piece into a sausage shape, about the diameter of a pound coin.

Cut each sausage into 2–3cm pieces.

Roll each piece on the back of a fork to create a ridged surface. This will help each gnocchi to hold more sauce.

Boil the gnocchi in salted water for about 3–4 minutes. You will know they are ready when they rise to the surface.

They can be eaten like this, but we prefer to fry them in butter to give them a fantastic golden colour and a deeper flavour.

Gnocchi goes brilliantly with this sweet and salty sauce, which James's Italian cooking mentor, Gianluca, showed us how to make. James spent a month in the Tuscan town of Lucca at his cooking school and we stopped off for lunch during our pilgrimage (knowing he usually has a trick and a bottle of wine up his sleeve). He made us this as it was pumpkin season, but you should definitely give gnocchi a try with your favourite pasta sauce or just a spoonful of pesto and a grating of Parmesan – it's easier than you think.

RICOTTA GNOCCHI WITH FENNEL SAUSAGE AND PUMPKIN

SERVES 4

TUSCANY

1 batch of our ricotta Gnocchi (see recipe on page 48)

For the sauce
Olive oil
350g Italian fennel sausages, skinned (a good deli should have these or use Cumberland sausages with an added teaspoon of fennel seeds)
1 onion, sliced into half moons
1 clove of garlic, finely chopped
500g pumpkin, peeled and cut into bite-sized pieces
Small handful of grated Parmesan, plus extra to serve
Sea salt and black pepper
Small handful of chopped parsley

Heat 2 tablespoons of olive oil in a medium saucepan and begin to fry the sausage, breaking it down into small pieces.

Once the sausage has taken on a little colour, add the onion and garlic and sweat for about 5 minutes until they have softened, but not coloured.

Next, add in the pumpkin, cover the pan with a lid and cook on a low/medium heat for 15–20 minutes until the pumpkin is tender.

Boil the gnocchi for 3–4 minutes in salted boiling water until they rise to the surface. Drain.

To finish, toss the gnocchi in the sauce with the grated Parmesan and season to taste with salt and pepper, adding extra olive oil if needed. Serve on warmed plates with extra grated Parmesan and the parsley.

There are two main types of pasta in Italy: a simple durum wheat flour and water pasta and a richer, egg-based pasta. Durum wheat is a very 'hard' grain with a high gluten content, which helps to bind the pasta and hold its shape while cooking, so there is no need for egg. This makes it better for drying and, more importantly, it's cheaper! In the North, they prefer to use a softer '00' flour that's finely milled and has a lower gluten content. This calls for the use of eggs to help strengthen the pasta and give a richer flavour. We prefer the '00' flour version as it has the richer flavour, a deep yellow colour and, let's be honest, as we run a pizza company, we have sacks of the finest '00' flour in Italy at our fingertips!

FRESH PASTA
ACROSS ITALY

SERVES 4–5

500g '00' flour
Pinch of sea salt
3 large eggs
2 extra egg yolks

Sift the flour onto a clean work surface and gather into a 'mound'. Create a well in the middle using your hand.

Sprinkle in the salt, followed by your eggs and yolks.

Using your fingers, lightly beat the eggs together before beginning to bring in the flour, bit by bit.

As you work in more and more flour, it should begin to come together to a stiff dough. It may seem like the dough won't take all of the flour, but keep going and it should all come together. If you are having real trouble, wet your hands and carry on.

Once the flour is completely incorporated and you have a smooth, springy but stiff dough, it's ready. It's important not to over-knead your dough as you can damage the proteins that give the pasta that all important 'al dente' texture.

Cover your dough with cling film and leave to 'rest' in the fridge for at least an hour (although overnight is better).

The pasta dough is now ready to be shaped...

Ahh pesto (not Bisto...). We both spent a good portion of our student years living off it. Pesto from a jar is still delicious, but it really pales in comparison to when it is made fresh. In Genoa, we met the man who grows the basil for the Pesto World Championships, Paolo Colcagno. While he wasn't looking, we got his girlfriend to show us his world-beating recipe for pesto. So here it is.

CLASSIC PESTO WITH FRESH ORECCHIETTE PASTA

SERVES 4–5

LIGURIA

For the pesto
1 small clove of garlic
Small handful of pine nuts, lightly toasted in a dry frying pan or under the grill
Sea salt
2 large handfuls of basil leaves
250ml olive oil
Small handful of grated Parmesan

For the orecchiette
1 batch of Fresh Pasta dough (see recipe on page 52)

Take your pestle and mortar and crush the garlic and pine nuts with a small pinch of salt until you have a rough paste. You can use a food processor here, but we much prefer the rougher texture you get with a pestle and mortar. So, with that decided, take your pestle and mortar and crush the garlic and pine nuts with a small pinch of salt until you have a rough paste.

Throw in your basil and begin to break it down (you may have to do this in two batches).

Begin to trickle in your olive oil until the basil has also come down to a rough paste and you have quite a loose sauce.

Stir in your Parmesan with a spoon and that's it.

To make the orecchiette, cut your pasta dough into six pieces and roll each piece into a sausage about the thickness of a 5p coin. Cut each sausage into 1cm pieces.

Take each piece of pasta and roll it on your work surface, under your thumb. This will create little orecchiette, which literally translates as 'little ears'.

Cook in a large pot of boiling salted water for 2–3 minutes or until they float to the surface. Serve the orecchiette with the fresh pesto.

Any leftover pesto can be spooned into an airtight sterilized jar (just immerse the jar in boiling water). It should be covered with a finger depth of olive oil and it'll keep in the fridge for 2–3 weeks.

This is everything that Italian food should be – colourful and packed full of flavour. Peperonata is hugely versatile and it can be stirred into pasta, served with meat or eaten cold as part of an antipasti plate. We first tried this on bruschetta at a little beach café in Calabria with a cold bottle of white wine and came to the conclusion that, without doubt, this was the best way to eat it. So here it is...

PEPERONATA ON BRUSCHETTA

SERVES 4

CALABRIA

Olive oil
1 onion, sliced into half moons
1 clove of garlic, chopped (optional)
1 red pepper, deseeded and sliced into 1cm strips
1 yellow pepper, deseeded and sliced into 1cm strips
2 bay leaves
6 plum tomatoes, roughly chopped
Sea salt and black pepper
Pinch of caster sugar
Small handful of basil
Squeeze of lemon juice
Ciabatta, to serve

Heat 3 tablespoons of olive oil in a large frying pan on a medium heat.

Sweat the onion in the pan for about 5 minutes until soft and translucent (this would also be the time to add your garlic if you wanted a heartier stew).

Add the peppers to the pan with the bay leaves. Cook down for a further 10 minutes until the peppers have softened.

Add the chopped tomatoes and season well with salt and pepper. Add the sugar to bring out the sweetness.

Cook on a low heat for 25–30 minutes with the lid off until you have a thick and rich stew. Add the basil leaves and lemon juice to finish.

Serve on toasted ciabatta with a little extra olive oil. Don't forget the wine and the beach.

OLIVE OIL

Do you know your virgin from your extra virgin? Or your biodynamic olives from your organic? Neither did we until we spent the day at an olive grove just outside of Lucca.

Giuseppe, the olive farmer, uses a biodynamic method to grow his olives. This involves some pretty scary concepts like burying cow horns filled with manure in the earth. Biodynamic farming really is a way of life, with the phases of the moon influencing when your fields need to be tended to, even if that means being up all night. The most important thing is that his olives, and the olive oil they produce, are top quality.

Once they have been harvested from the tree, using a machine called a manina, the olives are taken to the local press, which produces the oil for all the neighbouring farmers. We tasted some oil straight off the press and the first thing that hits you is how spicy the oil tastes. It almost makes you cough (see the YouTube video where Thom can barely get the words out after tasting it at www.youtube.com/pizzapilgrims). However, after it has been bottled, the spiciness disappears over time to leave the more familiar flavour that you only get from extra virgin olive oil.

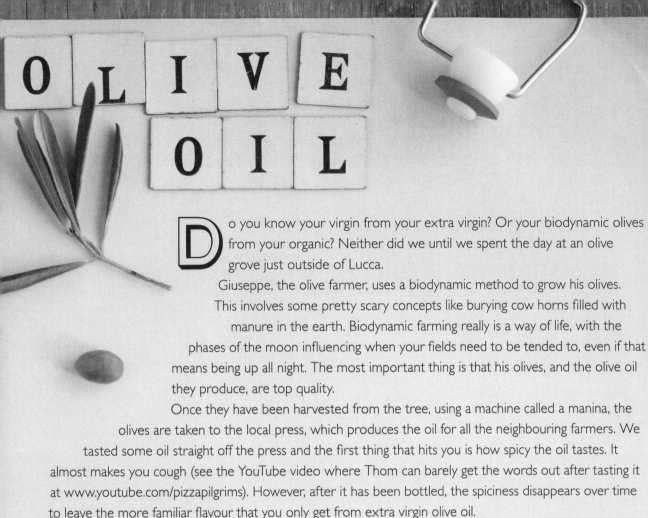

Which brings us on to the virginity question. This refers to which pressing of the olives the oil is extracted from. The first time the olives are pressed gives us extra virgin oil, but the pressed olives can be treated, heated and pulverized to get more and more oil out of them. This will have a lower quality and hence be virgin oil, or just plain oil.

See our recipes for flavoured oils you can make at home on pages 100–103.

Truffle oil is a great, affordable way to get the taste of truffle into your cooking. We put it on everything (mostly with pizza) but it definitely works best when combined with its cousin, the mushroom. The easiest way to make your own tagliatelle for this recipe is to use a pasta machine, but don't be put off if you don't have one – the Italians were making pasta for years before machines came around.

TAGLIATELLE WITH MUSHROOMS, CREAM AND TRUFFLE OIL

SERVES 4–5

TUSCANY

For the tagliatelle
1 batch of Fresh Pasta dough
  (see recipe on page 52)
  or 400g dried tagliatelle
Semolina, for dusting

If you have a pasta machine, you need to take your dough out of the fridge and, using a rolling pin, roll it out thin enough to fit between the rollers of the machine (about 1cm thick).

You start on the widest setting and work your way down. The trick is to fold the edges of the pasta into the middle (like a book) each time you run the dough through. This way you'll end up with a uniform sheet with straight edges.

If you're not using a machine, then simply grab your rolling pin and start rolling! Make sure you keep your work surface well floured and try to get as consistent a thickness as possible. If it takes you longer than 10 minutes, you're not working hard enough!

Once you've got it nice and thin (about the thickness of five sheets of paper), hang it over a broom handle or the back of a chair for about 15 minutes to let it dry slightly.

The pasta sheet will then take on a slightly leathery feel and will be easier to cut. Cut the sheet of pasta into rectangular sections, with one side about the same length as dried spaghetti.

Take each section and roll it up into a cigar shape. You can then slice it into 1cm strips that will uncurl into tagliatelle.

Lightly dust the pasta in semolina to prevent the strands from sticking together.

For the sauce
Olive oil
2 cloves of garlic, finely
  chopped
250g chestnut mushrooms,
  sliced (or any mushroom
  that takes your fancy)
25g dried porcini
  mushrooms, steeped in
  75ml water from the kettle
Glug of white wine
200ml double cream
Grated Parmesan
Small handful of chopped
  parsley
Sea salt and black pepper
Truffle oil (although it is
  expensive, a little goes a
  long way!)

Heat a couple of tablespoons of olive oil in a large frying pan.

Fry the garlic for about 30 seconds, then add the chestnut mushrooms just as the garlic begins to brown. Drain the porcini mushrooms (keeping the liquor), finely chop and add to the pan as well.

Once the mushrooms have taken on a little colour, add a glug of white wine and the mushroom liquor. Reduce down by half and then stir in the cream.

The tagliatelle should be cooked in a large pot of boiling, salted water for around 3 minutes or until it is tender but has a slight resistance under the tooth (AKA 'al dente').

Take the sauce off the heat, add your cooked pasta, a handful of Parmesan and the parsley. Season with salt and pepper to taste.

Serve with extra Parmesan and truffle oil.

It's rare that delicious things are also cheap, but mussels are exactly that. You can even get them for free if you live near the coast. This simple Neapolitan classic really makes them the star of the dish. The only boring bit is cleaning them up first, but settle in and have a beer — we promise it'll be worth it...

PEPPERED MUSSELS WITH LEMON

SERVES 4

CAMPANIA

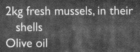

2kg fresh mussels, in their shells
Olive oil
2 cloves of garlic, finely sliced

Black pepper
½ a glass of white wine
Lemon quarters
Good bread, to serve

Clean the mussels by scrubbing under cold water, scraping away any barnacles and removing their beards. Discard any that are broken or open already and don't close when tapped.

Heat 2 tablespoons of olive oil in a large saucepan.

Fry the garlic until it begins to colour and then throw in the mussels.

Pepper is the big flavour in this dish, so you want to add around 20 twists of pepper (about a teaspoon).

Pour in the wine and cover the pan with a lid.

Cook for about 3 minutes, giving a good shake halfway through. The mussels are ready when they have all opened. Discard any that haven't opened.

Serve in a big bowl with an extra drizzle of olive oil, a quarter of lemon and some good bread.

This Sicilian dish could be the blueprint for southern Italian cooking: simple, inexpensive and packed with flavour. You can get frozen squid in the supermarket, but try getting fresh squid from your fishmonger. He'll do all the hard work for you and the flavour and texture is unrivalled. The rule with squid is always cook it hard and fast or long and slow. This stew is best left on the hob for a good hour, letting all the flavours develop. It's a great dish on its own with bread, but can also be used as a fantastic pasta sauce.

Calamari in umido
(Braised squid with tomatoes and chilli)

CAMPANIA

SERVES 4–5

1 onion
6 anchovy fillets
8 cloves of garlic, peeled and left whole
Olive oil
½ a glass of white wine
1kg cleaned fresh squid, the body cut into 2–3cm rings and the tentacles sliced in half
2 tins of San Marzano (or any good-quality Italian) tomatoes
Sea salt and black pepper
Handful of chopped parsley
Juice of 1 lemon
Good bread or spaghetti, to serve

In a large pan, gently fry the onion, anchovies and garlic in a couple of tablespoons of olive oil.

Once the onion has softened and the anchovies have dissolved, pour in your wine and reduce until the alcohol has cooked away.

Next, add the squid and cook for a couple of minutes before adding the tomatoes and salt and pepper to taste.

Turn down the heat and gently simmer for at least an hour, until the squid is soft and tender and the tomatoes have reduced to a rich sauce.

Stir through the parsley and lemon juice and check for seasoning.

Serve in a bowl with olive oil and good bread or with spaghetti.

BALSAMIC

Modena is famous for two things: Ferraris and balsamic vinegar. After spending a day at the Aceteria la Noce trying to learn how top-quality balsamic is made, we think we might have a better chance of knocking up a Ferrari on our own.

Balsamic production really is that complicated. A production line is made up of five barrels, each one slightly smaller than the last. The raw ingredient for balsamic is concentrated grape juice (called 'must') and the process is started by filling the first barrel with this sticky, sweet liquid. Each year, as the liquid evaporates, the ageing vinegar is used to top up the next smallest barrel down, and fresh must is used to fill the largest barrel. After 12, 18 or 25 years, the final product will be bottled from the smallest barrel in the chain and the topping-up process is repeated. It is a continuous, laborious and highly skilled process, which goes some way to explaining why a 100ml bottle of top-quality balsamic vinegar will sell for over £100.

When you taste the difference, though, you can really see why the people of Modena get so annoyed with the balsamic you find in the supermarket. The proper stuff is thick – almost treacly – and has a depth of flavour that you wouldn't believe. It can perk up pretty much any recipe and its amazing combination of sweetness and acidity really cannot be beaten.

Trattoria *Cenisio*

120L OF **MUST** (CONCENTRATED GRAPE JUICE).

5.

75L

OAK / CHESTNUT

Thinking about how badly some music, TV shows and clothes from 25 years ago have aged, the balsamic vinegar you can get today is basically the best advert the Eighties has...

TRADITIONAL BALSAMIC VINEGAR PRODUCTION.

As the liquid evaporates, each barrel is topped up with the liquid from the barrel before it.

BOTTLED BALSAMIC VINEGAR

4. 50L	3. 33L	2. 24L	1. 16L	5L

ERRY/OAK   JUNIPER   OAK   MULBERRY.

Every Italian thinks he makes the best minestrone. There are no rules, which gives everyone free rein to make it their own (and then put down everyone else's). It translates as 'big soup' and you don't get canvases much blanker than that! This particular recipe was made for us by Giuseppe, the chilli farmer we spent the day with in Calabria. Needless to say it packs a bit of a punch. That said, it is one of the most delicious versions we've tasted – great for clearing the sinuses in winter!

THE PEPERONCINO FARMER'S MINESTRONE

SERVES 4

CALABRIA

4 slices of pancetta
2 onions, roughly chopped
2 celery stalks, roughly chopped
2 carrots, roughly chopped
2 cloves of garlic, finely chopped
Sprig of thyme
Sprig of rosemary
1 bay leaf
Good pinch of peperoncino (dried chilli flakes)
1 tablespoon tomato purée
1 litre chicken stock
1 large potato, diced into 2–3cm cubes
Rind of a piece of Parmesan
2 good handfuls of orzo pasta
1 tin of cannellini beans
1 head of cavolo nero, shredded
Sea salt and black pepper
Good-quality extra virgin olive oil
Small ciabatta, sliced, toasted and rubbed with a clove of garlic, to serve

In a large saucepan, gently sweat the pancetta, onion, celery, carrot, garlic, herbs and (of course) the peperoncino for 10 minutes.

Add the tomato purée and cook for a further 5 minutes.

Pour in the stock and add your potato and Parmesan rind (this will add a great depth of flavour).

Simmer for 20 minutes until the potato is tender.

Add the pasta, cannellini beans and cavolo nero and simmer for a further 10 minutes.

Check for seasoning and add salt and pepper before serving in deep bowls with a trickle of good-quality olive oil and the toasted ciabatta rubbed with a garlic clove.

If you ever need a dish to impress your friends with, this is it. It looks incredible, but is actually very easy to pull off. The most important thing is getting hold of fresh seafood that is in season – after that it is hard to go wrong.

SHELLFISH WITH PARSLEY AND PEPPER CRUST

SERVES 4

CAMPANIA

A selection of shellfish
   (mussels, clams, king
   prawns, scallops etc.)
100g breadcrumbs
1 clove of garlic
Small handful of parsley
Grated zest of 1 lemon
Sea salt and black pepper
Olive oil
1 lemon, cut into wedges

First, clean your mussels and clams by scrubbing under cold water, discarding any that are broken or open already and don't close when tapped. Scrape away any barnacles from the mussels and remove the beards. Leave the clams for a couple of hours in clean water to get rid of any grit.

In a food processor, blitz together the breadcrumbs, garlic, parsley and lemon zest with a pinch of salt and pepper. Trickle in a tiny bit of olive oil to help loosely bind the breadcrumbs.

Leaving the shell on, halve the prawns lengthways and 'half shell' the clams, mussels and scallops.

Top each of your shellfish with some of the breadcrumbs and arrange in the remaining half of their shells on a large, flat baking sheet. Drizzle with olive oil.

Place under a hot grill for 3–4 minutes until the breadcrumbs have browned nicely and the meat is tender.

Serve with wedges of lemon and a cheffy flourish (whatever that is).

Caponata is one of the most flavourful dishes you can eat while also being (whisper it) quite healthy. Mixing fresh vegetables with capers and a sweet and sour sauce, it is delicious hot or cold and is really easy to make at home. To let you in on a little secret, the best caponata we have ever eaten was bought from a brilliant little deli in west London and consumed cold on a train to Newcastle with bread. If that doesn't show you that British veggies are as good as Italian, then nothing will. Amazing!

CAPONATA

SICILY

SERVES 4

2 small aubergines, cut into
  2–3cm chunks
1 onion, roughly chopped
2 celery stalks, roughly
  chopped
Small handful of capers
Big handful of green olives
  (stones out)
1 tablespoon caster sugar
1 tablespoon white wine
  vinegar
3 tablespoons tomato purée
Sea salt and black pepper

In a large saucepan, fry the aubergine (in batches so as not to overcrowd the pan) until golden. Set aside.

Sweat the onion and celery in the same pan on a low heat for 15–20 minutes until softened, but with no colour.

Add all the remaining ingredients and replace the aubergine, giving everything a good stir.

Put a lid on and cook for 15–20 minutes until you have a thick, rich stew.

PIZZA

This is where it all began for us. We originally set off to Italy to find out everything we could about pizza, and we certainly did that. We could have filled this whole book with detailed stats and information about gluten percentages and proving times – but we're not sure it would've been a real page turner. We did, however, pick up many, more interesting techniques, tips, tricks and recommendations, which is what this chapter is all about. Hopefully, we will have you making great Neapolitan pizzas, and their slightly more obscure cousins, in no time at all!

———

Pizza History

When we first had the idea to start our Pizza Pilgrimage, we were firmly of the impression that pizza is pizza. How many variations can there be? That was in the spring of 2011, and now, 18 months later, we couldn't have been more wrong. There was so much we didn't know, so much we have since discovered and even more for us still to find out. And what is most incredible is that even being one of the world's most popular foods, so few people are aware of what makes real Neapolitan pizza.

'PIZZA IS LIKE SEX, EVEN WHEN IT'S BAD IT'S GOOD'

Mel Brooks

And that's the problem. Whether it's delivered to you, eaten on the train, bought from a supermarket or even cold the morning after, we are evolutionarily disposed to like dough, cheese and tomato all cooked together.

It's because all pizza tastes good that there is never any reason to give it too much thought. This will all change the instant you try a great pizza. Not all pizzas – in fact very few pizzas – can really be considered great. And as soon as you try a great pizza, you really will struggle to go back to good pizza. It has, I'm afraid, turned us into 'pizza snobs', but we're actually OK with that…

OVER 5 BILLION PIZZAS ARE SOLD WORLDWIDE EACH YEAR.

When we think of pizza, we always think of Italy. However, the truth is that pizza is one of the most global foodstuffs this planet has to offer. From the Americas to the Middle East to Africa – the idea of a flatbread baked in the oven with toppings is not a uniquely Italian concept. And what is more, the Italians can't even truly lay claim to coming up with the idea first. Pizza has been eaten in some form for millennia and can be traced back to the ancient Greeks by even the laziest historian.

It was, however, the Italians who first started putting tomatoes on pizza when they arrived in Europe from the Americas in the late eighteenth century. Tomatoes were originally thought to be poisonous (which seems odd – why would you import something that you thought was poisonous?). It was the abject poverty around the port city of Naples that led people to use tomatoes on their baked bread out of desperation – and the first pizzas, as we know them, were born.

JUST BECAUSE IT'S FROM ITALY, DOESN'T MEAN IT'S GREAT.

Because pizza is so synonymous with Italy, it is a common mistake for people to think that every pizzeria in every region of Italy will always serve you a fantastic pizza. The truth is that the majority of the pizza you might find in northern cities like Milan, Turin or Venice will probably be no better than the standard pizza restaurant in London.

A visit to Rome or Naples, however, is a completely different story…

Napoli vs Rome — The Pizza War

This is the biggest contest there is in the world of pizza. This is dogs vs cats, Rocky vs Ivan Drago, The Stones vs The Beatles.

Both cities are internationally synonymous with pizza and in both you will find delicious, but very different, varieties. There is also a distinct difference in each city's attitude to pizza.

Neapolitan pizza

Pizza in Naples is a religion. As the city that lays claim to inventing the Margherita for the arrival of Queen Margherita of Savoy, they don't take pizza lightly. They have even campaigned for many years for the Margherita to gain UNESCO recognition on their 'intangible cultural heritage' list. The rules are many, and they are followed like a scripture by every Neapolitan pizzaiola worth his salt. Experimentation, with techniques, toppings or anything else, is highly frowned upon.

Neapolitan pizza is easily identified by its puffy crust, or cornicione, which will be 'leoparded' with charred spots bringing a smoky depth of flavour. The dough itself is soft, elastic and slightly chewy, making the crust something to cherish, not disregard like an unwanted KitKat Chunky wrapper.

Pizza is what brings the Neapolitan family together on a Sunday afternoon, in the same way an English family will cook up a roast. Come Sunday, the family will drop everything and all meet at their favourite pizzeria, catch up on the gossip, inevitably argue and share a Margherita.

Roman pizza

Romans treat their pizza with a touch more perspective than the Neapolitans. Don't get us wrong, people from Rome love their pizzas and would not settle for a bad one, but they are not as obsessed with it as the Neapolitans are.

Roman pizza actually comes in two distinct forms. The traditional variety has a paper thin, crispy base with toppings that go right to the edge. A slice of Roman pizza should be crispy enough to stay rigid when picked up.

The second variety has appeared in the last few decades and is called 'pizza al taglio'. This is cooked in large rectangular sheets, which are cut into square slices and sold by weight. The base of pizza al taglio is much thicker, almost like focaccia, but this variety is really about experimenting with new topping combinations. In that regard, the Romans have the exact opposite attitude to the experimentation-averse Neapolitans.

We visited the Pizzarium in the centre of Rome, where chef Gabriele Bonci makes some of the most far out but delicious pizza al taglio you can imagine. When we met him, he casually set light to a bunch of rosemary and then started stubbing out the flames on a pizza as he chatted to us. All in the pursuit of flavour...

THE NEAPOLITAN PIZZERIA

This is a picture of James in Da Michele in Naples, perhaps the most renowned pizzeria in all of Italy, if not the world. When Julia Roberts wasn't praying, or loving, she was eating pizza in this revered place. The locals refer to it as 'The Temple of Pizza', reflecting the near religious levels of respect pizza commands in the city. Luigi, standing in the photo here next to Thom, is the grandson of the man who claims to have invented the Margherita in the 1800s,

and the son of Michele (as in Da Michele). Safe to say, they know a thing or two about what makes a great pizza.

The truth is that there are a lot of pizzerias like Da Michele in Naples. Take a short walk down the Via Tribunali and you will pass some of the best in the business: Sorbillo, Del Presidente, Di Matteo – all right on top of each other. On our second trip to Naples we managed to put

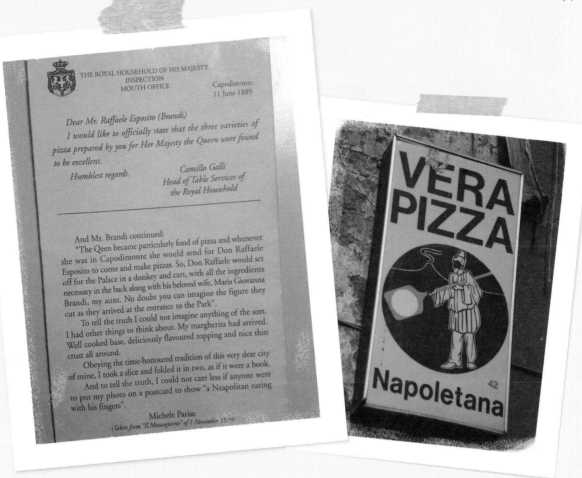

THE ROYAL HOUSEHOLD OF HIS MAJESTY
INSPECTION
MOUTH OFFICE

Capodimonte,
11 June 1889

Dear Mr. Raffaele Esposito (Brandi)
I would like to officially state that the three varieties of pizza prepared by you for Her Majesty the Queen were found to be excellent.

Humblest regards.

Camillo Galli
Head of Table Services of the Royal Household

And Mr. Brandi continued:
"The Qeen became particularly fond of pizza and whenever she was in Capodimonte she would send for Don Raffaele Esposito to come and make pizzas. So, Don Raffaele would set off for the Palace in a donkey and cart, with all the ingredients necessary in the back along with his beloved wife, Maria Giovanna Brandi, my aunt. No doubt you can imagine the figure they cut as they arrived at the entrance to the Park".
To tell the truth I could not imagine anything of the sort. I had other things to think about. My margherita had arrived. Well cooked base, deliciously flavoured topping and nice thin crust all around.
Obeying the time-honoured tradition of this very dear city of mine, I took a slice and folded it in two, as if it were a book.
And to tell the truth, I could not care less if anyone were to put my photo on a postcard to show "a Neapolitan eating with his fingers".

Michele Parise
(Taken from "Il Mezzogiorno" of 1 November 1930)

away 27 pizzas in 3 days between us (these work trips can be so demanding...). What is interesting is that they almost all claim to be the place where the Margherita was invented (although, if we are honest, Pizzeria Brandi seem to hold the strongest claim, and are certainly the only ones who are able to show any proof).

There is one organization that oversees all the pizzerias in Naples and sets the rules by which they must abide to be 'the real deal'. The Associazione Verace Pizza Napoletana (AVPN) is basically the Men in Black of the pizza world – secretive, in control and no nonsense. In the eyes of the AVPN you are not a pizzeria, and as such do not sell something they class as pizza,

unless you meet the criteria detailed in their eleven-page manual. ELEVEN PAGES – FRONT AND BACK! We won't go into them all here, but the key things to note are as follows:

+ The dough must rise for at least 12 hours.

+ The pizza must be cooked by a trained pizzaiolo with at least 2 years' training.

+ The pizza must cook for between 60 and 90 seconds.

+ You must use a traditional Pompeii wood-fired oven, reaching a temperature of 485°C.

As you would expect, they also have quite a bit to say about the ingredients you are allowed to use. Here is a quick summary:

Dough

The only four ingredients allowed in the dough are flour, water, yeast and salt. It's as simple as that.

The flour used must be '00' flour, which means it has been milled to the finest possible grade. The flour must also have a high gluten content (around 11–12 per cent).

Tomatoes

The tomatoes used must be the San Marzano variety, grown in the foothills of Mount Vesuvius just outside Naples. The tomatoes used on the pizza must not be cooked in any way prior to going in the oven – the sauce is purely pulped San Marzano tomatoes with a little salt.

Cheese

The cheese must either be mozzarella di bufala Campana (PDO) or fior di latte (a soft cow's milk mozzarella). Parmesan cheese is also used for added flavour.

This list of regulations goes on and on and in some (in fact most) places it just gets silly, detailing the pH the dough should be or how exactly the tomato sauce must be applied to the base.

And this, in our mind, is one of the biggest downfalls of the Neapolitan pizza. The rules are so thorough, and so strict, that there is no room for interpretation. No space for someone to come along and change things and put their spin on the classic. No thought for toppings that cannot be found in and around Naples.

TWO PIZZAS TO RULE THEM ALL

The AVPN only recognize two types of pizza: the Margherita and the Marinara. Take a look at the menu in Da Michele – these are the only two pizzas they serve.

Margherita sourdough base, San Marzano tomato, fior di latte, Parmesan, extra virgin olive oil, fresh basil.

Probably the most famous pizza there is and the one we would recommend to test out a pizzeria. If the Margherita is not good, then you can be pretty sure that all the pizza is going to be substandard.

Marinara sourdough base, San Marzano tomato, fresh garlic, oregano, fresh basil, olive oil.

The Marinara is fairly unique in the world of pizzas as it does not have any cheese on it. We have found on the market stall that this almost always puts people off, but it is probably one of our favourites as it packs in so much flavour. The name Marinara often leads people to think it has seafood on it, but it is actually so-called because it was eaten by people who worked at Naples' famous sea port.

MARGHERITA

MARINARA

NEAPOLITAN PIZZA DOUGH

This is the pizzaiola's signature, his pride, and a closely guarded secret that is, of course, always 'the best in Italy!' People try and overcomplicate the matter with bacterial cultures, leavening agents and oils in search of the perfect crust, but it really comes down to four things: the flour, the yeast, the temperature and time.

For the Neapolitan pizzaiola, the flour has to be '00'. This means that the wheat has been milled on the finest rollers, resulting in a 'talcum powder' soft flour that is completely pure with no husks. You are also looking for a high gluten content, for an elastic dough that catches air bubbles and gives a good rise to the crust. Our favourite flour is Caputo '00' Pizzeria flour, milled at the Molino Caputo, the largest flour mill in the heart of Naples. However, a good alternative with a high gluten content is strong Canadian bread flour, which can be found in the bigger supermarkets.

Fresh baker's yeast will add a greater depth of flavour and give a better rise than dry (the stuff you get in the sachets), as the process of drying yeast kills off a lot of the cells, leaving you with an unreactive and bland dough. You can find fresh yeast in the baking section of your local supermarket — just ask. Using cold water helps the dough to rise slowly, developing the flavour.

The most important thing is to let the dough rise slowly at room temperature (19–22°C) for a long time — 24 hours if possible. This will give you that deep 'beery' flavour that makes Neapolitan pizza so moreish.

MAKES 8 X 10 INCH PIZZA BASES
(each base is technically for one, but it's great sharing food)

1kg '00' flour with a high gluten content
2g fresh baker's yeast
600ml cold water
30g table salt

+ Tip the flour onto your work service and make a well in the centre. Dissolve your yeast in the water and pour into the middle of the well a little at a time whilst using your hands to bring the walls of the flour in so that the water begins to thicken. Once you've reached the consistency of custard, add the salt and bring in the rest of the flour until it comes together as a dough. Knead for 10–15 minutes.

+ Cover and leave to rest for 10 minutes before kneading again quickly for 10 seconds (this helps to develop the flavour and the gluten).

+ Divide the dough into 200g balls and leave to rest overnight or for at least 8 hours (24 hours is optimal, 48 hours maximum) in a sealed container or a deep baking dish sprinkled with flour and covered in cling film. Remember to leave space for each of your dough balls because, as the gluten relaxes, they will spread out to take up twice the diameter that they do initially.

+ After proving, the dough balls are ready to use straight away. We would recommend always making this amount of dough, even if you are only making pizza for a few people. There is a good chance you might want a second (or third, or fourth etc.) and pizza dough is actually fine to freeze once it has proved. Just defrost it in the fridge next time you want pizza — it's easier and quicker than ordering a takeaway!

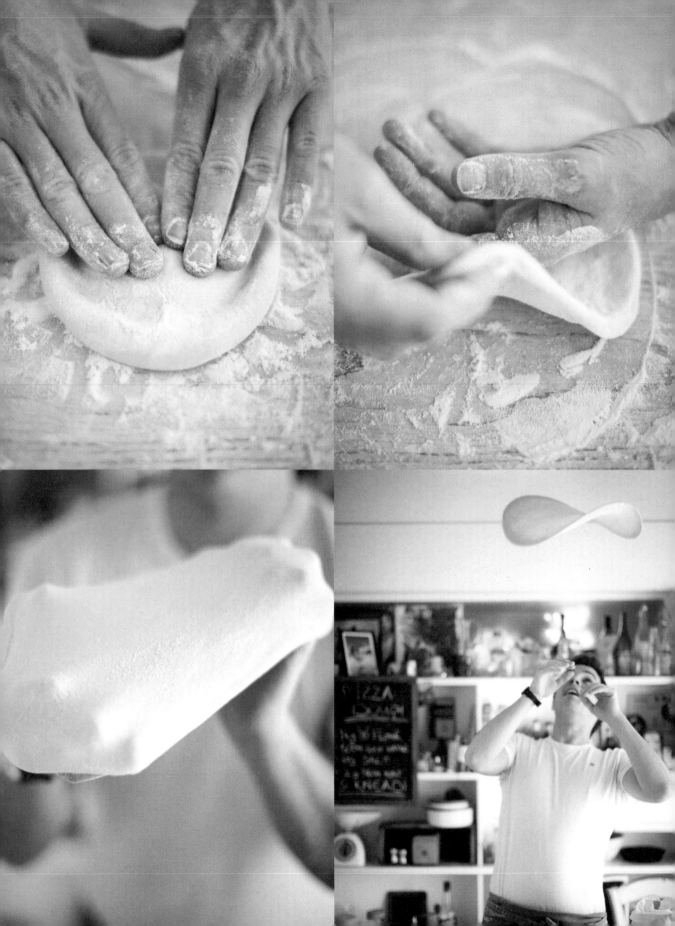

MAKING A PIZZA BASE

The trickiest part of making Neapolitan pizza at home is creating the base. It will take a bit of practice, and we guarantee your first few efforts will be a little misshapen, but making pizza is kind of like riding a bike. Once you have the knack, you never forget it.

The one thing to point out is that Napoli pizzaioli never, ever use a rolling pin. This is a cardinal sin in Naples, as it doesn't allow the crust of the pizza to be thicker than the centre. It's hands only – so take off those fake nails.

It's important not to overwork the dough or the gluten will tighten up and the ball will become unusable. One thing to mention is that you cannot reform a dough ball and have another go if you make a mistake – the only option is to start again with another ball.

❖ Scrape a dough ball out of its container using a spatula and as much flour as you need to ensure it doesn't stick. The rounder the dough ball comes out, the rounder the final pizza base.

❖ Put the dough ball onto a well-floured surface (honestly, if you are going to get serious about pizza making, get used to having flour play a large part in your life).

❖ Using your fingertips, press out the dough ball firmly, starting at the centre and working out to the edge. Ensure you leave a centimetre around the rim of the pizza untouched.

❖ Turn the dough ball over and repeat the pressing out process on the other side.

❖ Using the palm of your hand, do one firm push in the centre of the dough ball to ensure the thickness of the base is consistent (not counting the raised edges).

❖ Take the newly flattened dough ball on the back of your hands, ensuring the weight is on your knuckles and that your fingertips and nails are not going to poke a hole in the dough.

❖ Using the back of your hands, stretch the dough out as far as you can without tearing it (now there's a challenge). Turn the dough through 90 degrees and repeat this stretching. Do this a few times.

❖ You should now have a disc of dough around 10 inches in diameter, consistently thin but with a slightly thicker rim. We are ready to cook.

❖ Check out at our website (www.pizzapilgrims. co.uk) for more about making pizza.

❖ For the showman: try giving the pizza base a spin (making sure that someone is watching).

❖ With the dough still resting flat on your hand after stretching, turn your right hand palm-up. Clench your left hand into a fist.

❖ Twist your two hands in a clockwise motion while tossing the dough into the air with your right hand. Catch the dough on the back of your hands and repeat until you drop it.

❖ Take a fresh dough ball...

COOKING NEAPOLITAN PIZZA (THE MARGHERITA)

The fact of the matter is that the conventional oven you find at home will never be able to make a great Neapolitan pizza, even if the best pizza chef in the world was in charge of it. Most domestic ovens will only reach 250°C tops, and this is nowhere near the 500°C you would find in a domed pizza oven.

Luckily, there is a simple technique to try at home that uses equipment you will definitely have, unless you are a student. This method recreates the intense heat of a domed pizza oven and will put your conventional oven efforts to shame. The key thing to remember is the 'less is more' mantra of any Neapolitan pizzeria – too much cheese will result in a soggy, greasy mess.

MAKES 8 X 10 INCH PIZZAS

4 x balls of Neapolitan Pizza Dough
   (see recipe on page 80)
1 tin of San Marzano (or any good-quality
   Italian) tomatoes
A good pinch of sea salt
Grated Parmesan
A handful of basil leaves
150g fior di latte cheese (cow's milk
   mozzarella), torn into pieces no bigger
   than a 50 pence coin
Extra virgin olive oil

- Take the dough balls and press them out flat to make four 10 inch pizza bases using the tips of your fingers (see how to make a pizza base on page 83).

- To make the tomato sauce, first crush the tomatoes by hand. This stops the seeds being whizzed up by the blender, which makes the sauce bitter. Add a pinch of salt, then blitz with a hand blender until you have a tomato sauce with a slightly rough texture.

- Preheat the grill to its absolute highest setting.

- Lay a pizza base flat in a dry frying pan (preferably non-stick) that has been on a high heat and is screaming hot.

- Spread a thin layer of sauce with a ladle across the base, leaving a couple of centimetres round the edge for the crust. Add a pinch of Parmesan, basil leaves and a quarter of the mozzarella, in that order. Drizzle with olive oil.

- Once the base of the pizza has browned (about 1–2 minutes), take the frying pan and place it on the highest shelf, under the grill.

- Once the crust has taken on some colour (again about 1–2 minutes), the pizza is ready to go. Eat it fast (contrary to popular belief, pizza is not better cold the morning after!).

- Start making the next one…

BUILD YOUR OWN OVEN IN THE GARDEN

TO MAKE AN OVEN WITH A 90CM COOKING FLOOR

Wooden shipping pallets or something
  similar, to form a strong platform
1m x 1m sheet of MDF
15 insulating concrete blocks,
  to cover
1m x 1m when laid flat
45 firebricks
55 gallons building sand
17 gallons wet clay (either made
  from powdered clay to packet
    intructions or dredge it straight
    out of the ground – Catford on
     the River Thames is our favourite
     'dredging spot'!)
1 sack of straw
1 bag of sawdust (optional)

Another fantastic way to make pizza at home is to build yourself your own domed pizza oven. This is actually quite easy to do and will pretty much guarantee you a year's supply of DIY points around the house. You could quite easily start building the oven on Saturday morning and be up and cooking by Sunday lunch. We built the oven in this picture to make pizza at a friend's festival in about 3 hours out of some clay, a shipping pallet and a zinc galvanized bin…

Your garden pizza oven will be so much more versatile than that ropey old BBQ that's rusting in the shed. You can cook an amazing variety of things, from roasting joints to stews. You just have to be careful not to look too smug!

◆ First, stack the pallets on a flat surface to create a raised platform about waist height.

◆ Lay your sheet of MDF on the top of this platform and arrange your concrete blocks on top of it to create a solid 1m x 1m platform with no gaps.

◆ Lay your firebricks on top of the concrete blocks to create the oven floor. Again, no gaps here is essential to creating a smooth oven floor.

◆ Now, all those years of building sandcastles really pays off. Take the majority of the sand, wet it a little, and form a dome with a base around

90cm and a height of about 40cm. Make sure the dome is packed tight and has a smooth finish. Now wrap the dome with wet newspaper to create a smooth, solid structure.

◆ Mix your wet clay, sand and straw together, adding extra water if needed (you are looking for about 1 part clay, 2 parts sand and ½ a part of straw). The best way to create this mix is to put all the ingredients on a tarpaulin, take off your shoes and socks and crust it together with your feet (like making wine).

◆ Making the cob like this is not an exact science, but you are looking for a dough-like (very apt) paste that can be easily moulded to shape. You will know you have the right consistency when a ball of your mix sticks to your upturned palm.

◆ Add a layer of this clay mix on top of the newspaper-wrapped sand form. This layer should be about 15cm thick.

◆ Leave this layer of clay to dry overnight, making sure it isn't going to rain or that the oven is covered, but can still breath.

◆ The following morning, check that the mud layer has dried sufficiently (you should only just be able to dent it with you thumb). At this point, use a carving knife to cut a door in the front of the oven, about 45cm wide and 30cm high. Then carefully pull out the sand that made up the internal form.

◆ You should now be left with an empty oven (either that, or something has gone very wrong).

◆ Taking care, light a small fire in the oven with kindling and slowly build it up over the course of a few hours. This must be a slow process – you want to dry the oven out gradually to avoid cracks.

◆ After a few hours of burning, the oven is ready to use.

◆ You will find that the oven gets better with time as the residual moisture in the clay evaporates completely, allowing you to reach higher internal temperatures.

◆ If you are exceptionally adept around the house, you can look to add extra layers of insulation to your oven using a mixture of sawdust and clay. You can also build a basic structure and roof over it to protect it from the rain. Neither of these two are essential though (you will be pleased to know!). Your oven should happily last a year or two, just cover it with a tarpaulin during the winter.

COOKING PIZZA IN YOUR NEW OVEN

Once you are happy that the oven is ready, you can get started. It'll take a few thorough burnings of the oven before you can get up to full temperature, so perseverance is needed in order to get it performing at its best.

Getting started

First, light a fire. Channel your inner Ray Mears, starting with tinder and kindling. Once you have a good flame going, you can then start to add logs. Ideally use kiln-dried logs for the hottest possible flame and no spitting (you can buy kiln-dried logs at www.certainlywood.co.uk). Build the fire in the middle of the oven, to make it easier to manage, and then move it over to one side once it is up and running. The wood will smoke a little to begin with, but once the fire really gets going, the smoke should disappear. Get used to smelling of wood smoke for a few days after each firing – who needs Old Spice to smell manly?

Once the fire has burned for at least a couple of hours, the oven should be ready to take on a pizza. Sweep the cooking floor of the oven so that you don't end up with black-bottomed pizzas.

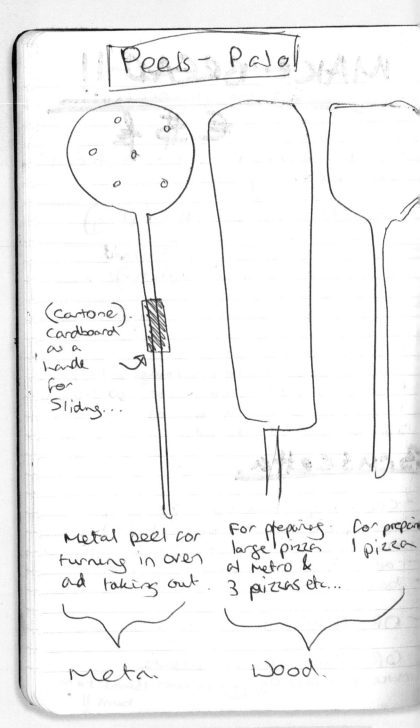

Peels - Pala

(cartone).
Cardboard as a handle for sliding...

Metal peel for turning in oven and taking out.

For preparing large pizza at metro & 3 pizzas etc...

For preparing 1 pizza

Metal.

Wood.

JAMES'S NOTEBOOK FROM THE TRIP

What tools you'll need

Turning the pizza is the hardest part of working with a wood-burning oven. The temperatures are so high that speed is often essential to stop the pizza burning to a crisp. You need two dedicated pizza peels – one for putting the pizza into the oven and one for turning the pizza and getting it back out. See James's drawings opposite.

The middle 'putting in' peel is ideally made of wood. You can buy them online or make one yourself from a piece of three-ply from Homebase.

The left 'turning' peel should be made of metal with a small circular head. Unfortunately, unless you are the DIY king, making one of these is really out of the question. They tend to be hard to track down, but you can buy them at www.nlce.co.uk.

For the 'amateur' pizzaiola, you can buy the peel on the right, a hybrid of the two, which will do the trick but gives you less control.

Making the pizza

Start by making the dough as on page 80 and then make your pizza base from it using the technique described on page 83. Sprinkle the wooden peel with flour. Place the base onto the peel and add the toppings as described on pages 90–98 (sorry about all the page turning).

Ensuring the pizza will move freely on the peel, place it into the oven. With the peel flat on the oven floor, slide the pizza off in one swift, confident move (like pulling a table cloth off a fully laid table).

After about 45 seconds (if the oven is at the right temperature), the pizza crust should have begun to puff up and the side of the pizza nearest the flame will have started to char. At this point, you need to turn the pizza through 180 degrees to make sure that it cooks evenly.

Take the second peel and carefully slide it under the base of the pizza on one side. Now, lift this side slightly off the floor of the oven and use the peel to spin the pizza around. This may take a couple of efforts before you get the knack (it certainly took us a fair few). The most important thing to remember is to return the pizza to the same spot on the oven floor once it has been turned, otherwise the exposure to a new area of hot floor will burn the base!

After another 30 seconds or so, the pizza should be ready to come out. If it's not quite there, with slight charring all around the edge, use the metal peel to 'dome' the pizza – raising it to the highest point in the centre of the oven where the heat is at its most intense. After 5 seconds, you will be ready to go.

There is no doubt that working with a wood-fired oven takes practice. Just make sure you don't invite anyone you really want to impress to your first-ever pizza party – probably don't invite any potential girlfriends/boyfriends until your fourth or fifth!

Great Neapolitan Pizza Toppings

(with inspiration from outside of Naples — gasp!)

SALSICCE E FRIARIELLI (SAUSAGE AND WILD BROCCOLI)

This is one of the most traditional 'bianca' pizzas that you will find in Naples (pizza without the tomato sauce). Salsicce here are Neapolitan fennel sausages, which must be pre-roasted in the oven. Friarielli is a kind of wild broccoli best bought in a tin, precooked in olive oil, chilli and garlic. Both can be found in good Italian delis.

The full ingredients are:
Grated Parmesan
Fior di latte cheese (cow's milk mozzarella)
Olive oil
Salsicce, roasted and cut into small pieces
Friarielli

92

Napoli salami

Napoli salami is a lightly smoked, cured pork sausage. It has a coarse texture and is studded with whole black peppercorns, which provide a bit of heat. It works brilliantly sliced thinly and placed on top of a Margherita (see recipe on page 85) before cooking. Forget pepperoni.

93

Filetti

This is another classic Neapolitan bianca pizza and a different spin on the Margherita. Take your pizza base and add a generous splash of olive oil. Sprinkle on some Parmesan and scatter with some halved cherry tomatoes. Finally, add some torn chunks of buffalo mozzarella and finish with some fresh basil leaves.

94

Salted courgettes with oregano and fresh garlic

Courgettes take time to salt, so it is worth preparing them when you're making the dough and storing both overnight. Slice the courgettes thinly (do yourself a favour and buy a mandolin, you will find yourself using it all the time and will only cut yourself the first three or four times you use it). Mix the courgettes with finely diced garlic, olive oil and a pinch of salt and dried oregano. Store in the fridge in an airtight container overnight. The next day drain off the excess liquid and add the courgette mix to the top of a Margherita before cooking.

94

Nduja

For serious spice lovers, this Calabrian sausage is perfect for pizza. Its soft, spreadable consistency means that it melts in the heat of the oven, leaving pools of spicy meaty goodness. Another ingredient that is perfect added straight to a Margherita before cooking. See page 139 for more info on nduja.

95

Romana/Napoletana
(warning: contains anchovies)

There have been presidential elections that have been less hotly debated than the greatest pizza question of all – anchovies or no anchovies? We are firmly in favour of our fishy friends and this combination of anchovies and capers added to a Margherita base is a winning combo for us. Weirdly, neither Rome nor Naples seem keen to claim this creation as their own. It's called Pizza Napoletana in Rome and Pizza Romana in Naples. They are probably concerned about the anti-chovy brigade coming after them.

96

Artichoke hearts with lemon and oregano oil

Artichoke hearts are an amazing combination of taste and convenience. They are one of the most delicious vegetables around and you can buy them in a tin all ready to go. They are perfect just drained and added straight from the tin onto a Margherita. A splash of our home-made lemon and oregano oil (see page 103) is the perfect complement, if we say so ourselves.

96

Fennel, ricotta and chilli

Ricotta's creamy texture is great on pizza and is perfectly complemented by the aniseed taste of the fennel. It took Thom a while to get over the slight sambuca flavour, but once you do it's a winner. This is another bianca pizza: spread the ricotta generously over the base, add a pinch of Parmesan, a drizzle of olive oil and sprinkle over finely sliced chilli and fennel (hello, Mr Mandolin!).

97

Prosciutto, Parmesan and rocket

Whatever you do, don't let prosciutto anywhere near your pizza oven. For this pizza, cook the Margherita as normal, then drape on slices of prosciutto, add some shavings of Parmesan (using a vegetable peeler) and scatter on some rocket leaves. This also works brilliantly if you replace the prosciutto with bresaola, a delicious cured beef from Lombardy.

98

Portobello mushroom and smoked garlic oil

This is a great combination and one of our bestsellers on the market stall. Mushrooms and garlic are an age-old pairing, and the smokiness of the oil adds depth to the overall flavour. You can see how to make the oil at home on page 100. These ingredients just need to be added to the Margherita toppings before cooking.

98

EATING NEAPOLITAN PIZZA

This may sound like a vaguely ridiculous or unnecessary section – everyone in the world knows how to eat a pizza.

However, given that they take it so seriously, it goes without saying that there are rules as to how you eat your pizza in Naples. Due to its doughy, not crispy, consistency, a slice of Neapolitan pizza cannot support its own weight like the hard men of the Roman pizza world. As such, there are a couple of approved methods that will stop you ruining that new white shirt.

The Napoli fold

Pizza is always served whole with a knife and fork in a Neapolitan pizzeria. If you are on a date, you will daintily eat your pizza in 'tiny little bites'. On the other hand, if you are with a friend, you cut it into four slices which can be folded in half (or even in three). These perfect pizza parcels can then be uncermoniously stuffed into your mouth without depositing toppings all over the table.

Pizza portafoglio

For those who want to eat their pizza on the move, or just for the plain greedy, Neapolitans have developed another way to eat their most famous creation: pizza portafoglio. Translating as 'pizza wallet', you take your freshly cooked pizza, without cutting it, and fold it in half and then in half again. This can be enjoyed on the go – but don't tuck in too vigorously as the cheese in the middle will be hotter than the sun!

FLAVOURED OILS
(GREAT WITH PIZZA, BUT GOOD WITH PRETTY MUCH ANYTHING!)

There are two main methods for infusing oils: hot and cold infusions.

Heating the infusion will help to release the oils from the 'flavour' ingredient. This is a quick process and you can have a good flavoured oil in a few hours. This is a great technique for more robust ingredients like spices or meats that benefit from being heated.

Cold infusion is better for more delicate flavours like herbs and garlic, where you want to retain their raw flavour.

Once you've made any of the oils below, store them in the fridge to keep them for longer.

Basil

This method will work with any delicate green herb from parsley to dill, but this basil option is our favourite. It is a great way to keep the colour of the herb you're trying to infuse.

Blanch a large bunch of basil leaves (about 100g) in boiling water for 10 seconds before shocking the leaves in ice-cold water. This will help to set the chlorophylls and retain the bright green colour in the oil.

Blend the basil in a food processor with 750ml olive oil and then leave to infuse for a couple days.

Strain the oil and bottle in airtight sterilized bottles (just immerse them in boiling water).

Smoked garlic

This is a little bit of a DIY project, but it's definitely worth giving it a try because what you end up with is essentially 'bottled smoke', which pretty much goes with anything!

Take a metal tin (a Quality Street tin is perfect) and punch a few holes in the lid with a screwdriver.

Punch four holes in the sides of the tin, halfway up, at 3, 6, 9 and 12 o'clock. Thread metal wire through the holes and tie so that you're left with a cross through the middle of the inside of the tin. This will act as your shelf to hold a round cake cooling rack that you can buy from a cooking shop for about £4.

Fill the bottom with a couple of centimetres of wood chips (oak or hickory are good). Taking great care, light with a blowtorch and then place your shelf on top of the wires, littered with whole garlic bulbs.

Place the lid on the tin and leave to smoke (outside!!) for an hour or two.

The garlic bulbs should come out looking much darker in colour and with an incredible garlic smokiness.

Put three heads of the garlic in a sterilized airtight container with 750ml olive oil and leave to infuse for a week (2 weeks is better). This oil is fine kept out of the fridge for a couple of weeks, but if you want to keep it for a long time, then do store it in the fridge.

BASIL

SMOKED
GARLIC

CHILLI

OILS

NDJUA

ANCHOVY

LEMON
AND
OREGANO

Chilli

You can just add dried chillies (see our tips on page 45) to olive oil and leave it to infuse for a couple of weeks, but we prefer this method as you get more of the chilli flavour, not just the heat.

Place an ordinary olive oil, or flavourless oil of your choice, in a pan with as many dried chillies as you're brave enough to add (we use about five bird's eye chillies and prefer dried as it gives a warmer, smokier flavour).

Put the pan on a medium heat and, using a thermometer, heat the oil to 60–70°C.

Keep at this temperature for 4–5 minutes, then take off the heat and leave to cool for a good couple of hours.

Strain the oil and bottle in airtight sterilized bottles (just immerse them in boiling water).

Nduja

A nice meaty alternative to chilli oil, nduja (see page 139) gives this concoction the most incredible colour.

Break up 400g nduja into a saucepan and render down over a medium heat until it has completely melted.

Fry for 3–4 minutes until the meat begins to gently caramelize before pouring in 700ml olive oil, taking off the heat and leaving to cool and infuse for a couple of hours.

Strain the oil and bottle in airtight sterilized bottles (just immerse them in boiling water).

Anchovy

The idea of this oil will either fill you with dread or ecstasy!

In a saucepan, bring 750ml olive oil up to 60–70°C with 100g tinned anchovies in oil.

Keep at that temperature for 10–15 minutes before taking off the heat and leaving to cool and infuse for a couple of hours.

Blend the oil and anchovies in a food processor before straining and bottling in airtight sterilized bottles (just immerse in boiling water).

Lemon and oregano

A really fresh tasting oil, this is our tribute to the mild sauce in your favourite high-street chicken restaurant. Although that is probably cheapening it a little...

Wash and zest a lemon using a sharp paring knife or vegetable peeler. Make sure you only take the yellow part of the zest and not the white pith.

Heat the zest with 750ml olive oil at 60–70°C for 4–5 minutes before taking off the heat and leaving to infuse for a couple of hours or more.

Pour the oil and zest into airtight sterilized bottles (just immerse the bottles in boiling water) and add a generous sprig of good-quality dried oregano to each one. Leave to infuse for 1–2 weeks before using.

Pizza variants using Neapolitan dough

The term 'calzone' comes from the Italian word for a trouser leg. Now we've never actually tied a knot in a pair of old trousers and stuffed it with tomatoes and ricotta, but we get the sentiment. A calzone actually has a very different flavour to a normal flat pizza as the dough protects the rest of the ingredients from the dry heat of the oven, resulting in a sweeter, more delicate taste.

Classic Neapolitan Calzone

CAMPANIA

MAKES 4 CALZONE

4 x balls of Neapolitan Pizza Dough (see recipe on page 80)
8 tablespoons tomato sauce (see recipe on page 85)
250g tub of ricotta cheese
Grated Parmesan
2 balls of buffalo mozzarella
12–16 basil leaves
Olive oil

Put your oven on full whack (around 250°C/230°C fan/Gas 9).

Take the dough balls and press out flat to make four 10 inch pizza bases using the tips of your fingers (see how to make a pizza base on page 83).

Spread the tomato sauce over one half of each base.

Dot large blobs of the fresh ricotta over the tomato and sprinkle with a pinch of Parmesan.

Tear over some buffalo mozzarella and add the basil leaves.

Drizzle over a little olive oil and fold the pizza bases in half, pressing down the edges to create a good seal.

Dab the calzones with a little olive oil and finish with some more Parmesan before baking in the oven for 10–12 minutes.

Scacciata (Sicilian calzone)

This is the Sicilian cousin of the Classic Neapolitan Calzone above. It's prepared in the same way, but stuffed with broccoli, onions, mozzarella and maybe some sausage (but often not, as it was traditionally a peasant food).

Fogotto are little sacks, made by taking the four corners of a sheet together and slinging them over your shoulder (like a cross between a Dick Whittington sack and a Father Christmas sack). It is also where these little pizza dough packages get their name. They are a really simple twist on normal pizza and great for little canapés.

Fogotto
(Little Pizza Sacks)
CAMPANIA

MAKES 4 FOGOTTO

½ a lemon
½ an orange
½ handful of walnuts
4 tablespoons ricotta cheese
Sea salt and black pepper
1 x ball of Neapolitan Pizza
    Dough (see recipe on
    page 80)

Put your oven on full whack (around 250°C/230°C fan/Gas 9). You want to give it a good hour to get its act together.

Using a cheese grater, take off the zest of the lemon and the orange, being careful not to get any of the bitter white pith under the skin.

Crush the walnuts using the classic stress-relieving method of wrapping them in a clean tea towel and smashing them to bits with a rolling pin.

Combine the crushed walnuts, zests, ricotta and seasoning in a bowl.

Take a proved dough ball and divide it into four small dough balls.

Flatten out each of these small balls to create a mini pizza about 12cm in diameter and 6–7mm thick.

Place a tablespoon of the ricotta mixture in the centre of each circle of dough.

Now, carefully fold each of the four corners of the mini pizzas into the centre and crimp them together in one central point (we know a circle doesn't have corners, but hopefully that makes sense). When you fold in the corners, it will make four natural seams that you should leave open to allow the steam to escape and let the heat of the oven in.

Place the fogotto on a baking tray and bake in the oven for 10–12 minutes.

We spent an afternoon in the infamous Spanish Quarter of Naples, where tourists fear to tread! Here we met two sisters who, at 5pm every Friday, open up their little shop and sell traditional 'pizza fritta', or deep-fried pizza, to the locals. This couldn't be further from the abominations found in Scottish chip shops (look up 'pizza crunch' online and prepare to be appalled). This is light, slightly crispy and a pretty perfect demonstration of a good pizza dough. Don't get us wrong: it will probably shave a year or two off your life, but in the tastiest possible way!

PIZZA FRITTA

CAMPANIA

MAKES 2 PIZZA FRITTA

2 x balls of Neapolitan Pizza Dough (see recipe on page 80)
4 tablespoons tomato sauce (see recipe on page 85)
1 teaspoon grated Parmesan
2 slices of prosciutto cotto (cooked ham)
1 x ball of buffalo mozzarella
Few dollops of ricotta cheese
Groundnut, sunflower or vegetable oil, for deep-frying

Take the dough balls and flatten them out, using your hands or a rolling pin, to a 25–30cm diameter, about 6mm thick.

Spread the tomato sauce onto one half of each pizza base.

Sprinkle with grated Parmesan, tear over the slices of ham and the mozzarella and add a couple of small dollops of ricotta cheese to each one.

Fold the pizza bases over and press firmly along the edge to make a good seal.

Heat the oil to 180°C (if a cube of bread browns in 15–20 seconds, the oil is hot enough). Taking care with the hot oil, deep-fry each pizza for 3–4 minutes, turning halfway through so that they colour and cook evenly.

Drain on kitchen paper and eat immediately, defibrillator at the ready...

This pizza actually originates from Nice, a town that has spent a fair chunk of time fluctuating between being part of Italy and part of France. This has rubbed off on its food, leaving a real combination of Italian and French cooking. Controversially, it features no cheese and no tomato ('Lunacy!' we hear you cry), but stick with us — it is worth it.

Pizza all'Andrea or Pissaladière

SERVES 4—6

NICE, FRANCE

1 or 2 x balls of Neapolitan Pizza Dough (see recipe on page 80)
3 large onions, sliced
2 cloves of garlic, finely chopped
Olive oil
Anchovy fillets
Black olives (stones out)

Preheat the oven to 200°C/180°C fan/Gas 6.

Roll out your pizza dough and line a deep, circular baking dish. You may need to combine two dough balls to cover the entire dish.

In a frying pan on a medium heat, sweat down the onion and garlic in olive oil. You want to get a deep brown colour on the onion, making sure that it does not burn (obviously).

When the onion is ready, arrange in the baking dish on top of your dough and flatten the pile down into the dish.

Lay the anchovy fillets on top of the onion in a crisscross layout.

Stud the olives in the gaps between the anchovy crosses.

Bake the pizza for around 20 minutes until the base is golden and crispy.

Enjoy — but given the amount of garlic and onion, make sure you brush your teeth before heading out the door!

Antonino Esposito really is our Mr Miyagi of pizza. We spent an afternoon with him in the town of Sarno cooking in his awesome outdoor pizza oven. In those few hours, we learned more about pizza than anywhere else in Italy. He takes pizza pretty damn seriously – his all-black business card describes him as an 'Executive Pizza Chef' in silver raised lettering. Patrick Bateman, eat your heart out. These bocconcini are like little pizza Chelsea buns and were one of our favourites of Antonino's many creations.

BOCCONCINI DI PIZZA
(A PIZZA CHELSEA BUN)

SERVES 4

CAMPANIA

1 x 500g ball of Neapolitan Pizza Dough (see recipe on page 80)
4 tablespoons tomato sauce (see recipe page 85)
Grated Parmesan
Small handful of basil leaves
1 x 125g ball of buffalo mozzarella
6–8 slices of prosciutto
Olive oil

Preheat your oven to 250°C/230°C fan/Gas 9.

Stretch (or roll) out your dough ball into a large rectangle (approx. 60cm x 30cm).

Spread the tomato sauce over the dough and sprinkle with the grated Parmesan, basil leaves and small pieces of mozzarella.

Take the slices of prosciutto and lay them flat, in a line, on top of the dough.

Starting at the long edge, roll the dough up (like a roulade), sealing at the end with a dab of water on the edge of the dough.

Cut off 5cm thick slices and pack, cut side up, on a well-oiled baking tray. Make sure the rolls are tightly packed together on the tray.

Sprinkle with a little extra Parmesan and a drizzle of olive oil.

Bake in a hot oven for 20–30 minutes until the dough is cooked through and the tops have taken on some colour.

The bocconcini should pull apart into individual 'Chelsea bun-esque' portions.

Saltimbocca translates as 'jumps in the mouth', which this recipe does not literally do (that's science fiction territory). It is, however, the place where pizzas and sandwiches meet – an excellent combination, we're sure you'd agree. It's not possible to make these in a conventional oven at home, so these will need to be a little reward for those who have built their own oven (see pages 86–87). Gold star for you guys. Anyone else, I'm afraid you will have to pop down to Pizza Pilgrims and we will rustle one up for you. (Apologies for the shameless plug...)

SALTIMBOCCA
(PIZZA SANDWICHES)
CAMPANIA

2 x balls of Neapolitan Pizza Dough (see recipe on page 80)
Fior di latte (cow's milk mozzarella)
Napoli salami, thinly sliced
Basil

Take two proved pizza dough balls and flatten them into an ellipse (oval) shape, ensuring you flatten all the way to the edges.

Taking one ball, place a hand at each end of the oval and shuffle the dough back and forth on the work surface to stretch it out even further. You are looking for a piece of dough that is flat all the way to the edge and about three times longer than it is wide. Repeat with the other ball.

Using a pizza peel, put one piece of dough in the coolest part of the pizza oven. Watch in awe – it will puff up like a balloon in front of your eyes (simple things for simple minds).

Flip the puffed-up dough over and let it take colour on the other side.

Take the saltimbocca pocket out of the oven and cut it open down one side.

Fill the pitta-bread-style pocket you have created with the fior di latte, salami and basil.

Return the saltimbocca to the oven until the cheese has melted. Start the next one…

Obviously, being a take on the sandwich, feel free to experiment with any combination of fillings that take your fancy.

For anyone who only has access to a conventional oven, try our Piadina recipe on page 122 instead.

SWEET PIZZA TOPPINGS USING NEAPOLITAN DOUGH

Sweet pizza – or sweetza as we call it – divides opinion like Lady Gaga. Some think it is just a gimmick, while some see genius in the combining of things that shouldn't really go together. We are firmly in the latter camp (on sweetza, not Lady Gaga) and think that salty pizza dough combined with sweet toppings and fillings is a winning combination. Just don't mention it to any Neapolitans and you will be fine!

Tocchetti (deep-fried pizza fingers)

Take a dough ball (from the batch of our Neapolitan Pizza Dough on page 80 that you've, of course, already made) and cut it into strips, each about the size of a marker pen. Heat the oil to 180°C (if a cube of bread browns in 15–20 seconds, the oil is hot enough). Taking care with the hot oil, deep-fry the strips until golden brown. Once cooked, take out of the oil, drain on kitchen paper, then roll in caster sugar and ground cinnamon. Eat straight away or dip them in Nutella for an extra sugar hit.

Peach and cinnamon 'peachza' with cream

This is definitely not in the authentic 'Pizza Bible', but peaches, cinnamon and cream is a classic Italian combo and works so well on a pizza. De-stone and roughly chop two of the ripest peaches you can get your hands on. Place in a bowl, squeeze over the juice of a lemon, a good tablespoon of sugar and a level teaspoon of ground cinnamon. Give it a good mix and leave it for at least an hour (or overnight is better) to macerate. Spread generously on a pizza base and drizzle with cream before baking.

Nutella and ricotta calzone

We saw this a lot throughout Italy and we were shocked at how dearly Italians hold Nutella to their hearts. To be fair, it is freaking delicious! Warm the jar of Nutella in a pan of hot water to make it easier to work. Spread a good tablespoon of it on one half of a pizza base and dot with little dollops of fresh ricotta. Fold the pizza in half and press along the edges to make a good seal before baking for 4–5 minutes in the oven at 250°C/230°C fan/Gas 9. Once out of the oven, drizzle over a little more Nutella and dust with icing sugar. This recipe is also worth trying with our Roast Chestnut and Dark Chocolate Spread on page 21.

Unlike Neapolitan pizza, al taglio can be cooked in a conventional oven, which makes it ideal for cooking at home. What's more, it's a great way of using up anything you have left in the fridge from the night before (which you can later pretend was a combination that you had been perfecting for months). Creativity in the toppings is positively encouraged, so push the boat out and experiment.

PIZZA AL TAGLIO DOUGH AND TOPPINGS

SERVES 6–8

LAZIO

For the dough
800ml lukewarm water
1g dried yeast
1kg plain or wholemeal
  bread flour
20ml sunflower oil
20–25g table salt

For the tomato sauce
1 tin of San Marzano (or
  any good-quality Italian)
  tomatoes, crushed
Glug of olive oil
Pinch of sea salt
Squeeze of tomato purée

Suggested topping combos
Nduja and thinly sliced fennel
Courgette flowers and
  anchovies
Grilled aubergine and
  Gorgonzola
Cherry tomato, shaved
  Parmesan and rocket
Roast pumpkin purée,
  mozzarella and fried sage
Mozzarella, capers, anchovies,
  black olives and sun-dried
  tomatoes

Mix the lukewarm water and the yeast together until dissolved.

Add the flour, oil and salt and knead until you have a wet, sticky dough.

Leave the dough covered for 24 hours to rise and prove.

The next day – when you are ready to eat – get the oven on full whack to 250°C/230°C fan/Gas 9. Ideally you want to give the oven a good hour to heat up.

Take the risen dough, knock it back and then roll it into a large rectangular shape.

Place your dough in a large, heavy-bottom baking tray.

Top the uncooked dough with the uncooked tomato sauce (made by mixing the ingredients listed together). Leave a 1cm rim uncovered to create a crust.

Cook the pizza for 10 minutes, then take it out of the oven. This is the fun bit.

Add the toppings, either following some of our suggestions or coming up with your own creations. The more weird and wonderful the better. Return the pizza to the oven for another 10 minutes.

Get the pizza out of the oven and then cut it up as you see fit. Make sure you get one of the corner bits!

This is the other famous Roman pizza: a thin and crispy base, known in Italy as 'scrocchiarella', with a good covering of toppings. This is probably closest to what most British people imagine when they think of a pizza. The opposite to a Neapolitan style, the crust should be almost non-existent with cheese and tomato right to the edge and no cornicione in sight. These pizzas will work perfectly with the topping combinations listed in the Neapolitan pizza section.

THIN CRUST 'SCROCCHIARELLA' ROMAN PIZZA DOUGH

LAZIO

MAKES 5 PIZZA BASES
(or 2 single person pizzas + one big thick one)

1 x 7g sachet dried yeast
1 teaspoon sugar
300ml lukewarm water
500g '00' flour
2 tablespoons olive oil
Good pinch of sea salt

Whisk the yeast and sugar into the lukewarm water and leave it to sit at room temperature for about 15 minutes until a foam has formed on the top.

Pour the flour onto a clean work surface and, using your hand, make a well in the middle.

Pour in the yeast mix, olive oil and salt a little at a time whilst bringing the sides of the walls in with your fingers.

Once the dough has come together, knead well for 10–15 minutes until you have a smooth and springy dough. Cover with a damp cloth and leave to rest for 20 minutes.

Divide the dough into 200g dough balls, cover again and leave to prove for an hour until they have almost doubled in size.

The dough balls are now ready to use, but can be kept in the fridge for a few hours if needed.

Either hand stretch the dough on a well-floured work surface or use a rolling pin to get an evenly thin pizza base – about 2–3mm is perfect.

V. v good. Definitely do this one again! :) Thin + slightly puffs up round the edges

SOME FAMOUS ROMAN PIZZERIAS

Li Rion

One of the most popular pizzerias in town, not least because it is right by the Colosseum and feeds the hordes of tourists that turn up every day. Without doubt the best pizza here is the Margherita with Spianata Romana, a delicious Roman salami, studded with black peppercorns.

Da Remo

The place to get the most traditional 'scrocchiarella' Margherita pizzas – simply tomatoes, basil and mozzarella on an impossibly thin and crispy base.

La Fucina

A newcomer to the Rome pizza scene, this place specializes in more adventurous toppings, and the pizzas come out one by one so everyone round the table can share and try each one. Our favourite was the mortadella and pistachio pizza.

Sforn

Often tipped as Rome's best pizzeria, they do a great pecorino and black pepper pizza on a bianca (no tomato) base. It's a little nod to the classic Roman dish Cacio e Pepe (see recipe on page 148).

Monte Carlo

The queue out of the door here is testament to the quality of their pizzas. We spent a full day here learning the tricks of the thin-crust Roman pizza trade – and their collection of 'celebrity' photos is pretty impressive, too.

Pizzarium

Pizza al taglio from chef Gabriele Bonci, a true pizza maverick. He let us into his kitchen for an afternoon and showed us the ropes on pizza al taglio – the recipe in the book comes from him.

It makes sense that piadina hails from the Emilia-Romagna region of Italy. Piadina is basically just a wrapper for as much cheese and cured meat as you can fit into it. Between Parma and Reggio, they certainly produce a lot of both. Piadinerie (piadina kiosks) are dotted across the region with the regularity of Starbucks and at any hour of the day you will see people waiting in line for their piadina fix. They are super simple to make at home and, like most sandwiches, they are all about the filling.

PIADINA
(ITALIAN FLATBREADS)
EMILIA-ROMAGNA

MAKES 4 PIADINA

For the piadina bread
500g white '00' flour
75g lard or vegetable oil
5g sea salt
Pinch of bicarbonate of soda

Some suggested piadina fillings
Parma ham, mozzarella and
    rocket
Sun-dried tomato paste,
    chargrilled courgettes and
    Parmesan
Fried sliced aubergine and
    stracchino cheese
Peperonata (see recipe on
    page 56) and goat's cheese
Pesto (see our recipe on
    page 55), mozzarella and
    tomato

Add the flour, lard, salt and bicarbonate of soda to a mixing bowl. Slowly add 200ml water and combine all the ingredients with your hands.

Once you have a workable dough, take it out of the bowl and knead it until smooth on a floured work surface.

Place the dough in a covered bowl and leave it for at least 30 minutes to rise in a cool place (as there is no yeast, it is the bicarbonate of soda doing all the work, so temperature is not an issue).

Divide the dough into four. Work each of these into a round ball, then roll each one out to a 25cm flatbread with a floured rolling pin.

Get a dry frying pan on a high heat and wait for it to come up to temperature. Place a piadina into the pan.

Use a fork to prick the flatbread all over and stop bubbles of air forming. Once the first side has taken some colour, flip the piadina over. Press down any bubbles that do start to form with the back of the fork.

Add the filling to the piadina while it is still in the pan, then fold in half. Toast for 1 minute on each side, or until the cheese has melted.

WALTER SANTESSO e MAGALI NOËL

Gaeta is a little fishing town on the coast between Naples and Rome that holds the honour of being where the word 'pizza' was first recorded, back in 977. Tiella is a small pie, made from pizza dough and stuffed full of whatever is local and in season. We arrived just as octopus was coming in on the local fishing boats, so it was straight out of the sea and into the pie. Tiella is Gaeta's answer to the doner kebab, with the little takeaway shops on the beach packed until the early hours with people who may have had that one Birra Moretti too many.

TIELLA DI GAETA (SEAFOOD PIE)

SERVES 6

LAZIO

1kg cleaned octopus (get your fishmonger to gut and clean your octopus, otherwise ink will go everywhere and I can vouch that it doesn't come out of jeans!)

4 tablespoons extra virgin olive oil

2 large cloves of garlic, sliced

2 bay leaves

1 tin of San Marzano (or any good-quality Italian) tomatoes (break them up with scissors)

Large handful of stoned black olives

Pinch of peperoncino (dried chilli flakes)

Big pinch of sea salt and black pepper

Small handful of chopped parsley

1 x large dough ball, 300g from the Neapolitan Pizza Dough recipe (see page 80), but cut the flour with 30% semolina flour – it gives the dough a deeper flavour and a firmer texture

Boil the octopus for about 35 minutes or until tender (you should be able to pierce it easily with a knife but still feel some resistance), leave to cool in the water and then chop into pieces about the size of your thumb nail.

Heat 2 tablespoons of olive oil in a frying pan, add the garlic and cook until it begins to turn golden.

Add the octopus and bay leaves and fry for another minute. Next, add the tomatoes, olives and peperoncino flakes.

Season with salt and pepper and cook for 5 minutes to let the tomatoes reduce to a thick sauce. Add the parsley and leave the whole thing to cool (overnight will make it taste even better).

To assemble the pie, first preheat the oven to 230°C/210°C fan/Gas 8.

Take your pizza dough and roll it out to the thickness of a pound coin. Then line an oiled shallow dish with half the dough, just like you would a normal pie, leaving about 1cm overlapping the edge.

Pour in your filling and make sure you really pack it in as you don't want any air bubbles.

Roll out the remaining dough into a thin circle (about 1cm thick) and place on top, cutting off the excess and leaving a 1cm lip for crimping.

In Gaeta, everyone who's anyone has their own crimping style for their Tiella. It's important to create a good seal as you don't want any of the juices leaking out, so ensure the edges are pressed together firmly (like a Cornish pasty). Cut a small steam hole in the centre and drizzle the remaining olive oil over the top.

The whole thing then goes into the oven for about 40 minutes or until you have a deep golden crust.

PARMESAN

Parmesan cheese is one of the most enduring culinary exports that Italy has to offer. Its full name, Parmigiano Reggiano, is derived from the two towns it is most closely associated with: Parma and Reggio Emilia. Parmesan is held in such high regard in these towns that you are able to use wheels of it as collateral against a bank loan!

Despite only calling for three ingredients (milk, rennet and salt), Parmesan production is extremely complicated once you get down to the nitty gritty.

Milk is delivered to the factory twice a day where the master cheese maker oversees blending and cooking the milk for the production of every individual Parmesan cheese. He is only paid for the ones that end up passing the stringent tests after months of curing, so it's in his interest to stay focused.

Parmesan that you buy in the shops is usually distinguished by the number of years it has been aged for. There are three main varieties: one, two or three-year aged. The cheese cannot be referred to as Parmesan until it's at least one year old!

The older the cheese, the more intense the flavour, with three-year Parmesan said to taste of leather and spices! The cheeses are stored in huge maturing rooms, which often contain up to 25 thousand wheels of cheese – with a market value of 10 million euros!

Here are a few fun Parmesan facts to leave you with:

- During the production process, the lactose in Parmesan is converted to lactic acid. This means it's suitable for those who are lactose intolerant!
- Older Parmesan has visible white deposits, which bring a crumbly, slightly crunchy texture. These are broken down proteins, which make Parmesan a great food for active sportsmen, as the body can quickly absorb them.
- As Parmesan is made with unpasteurized milk, it is illegal to sell it or produce it in many countries, including Australia.

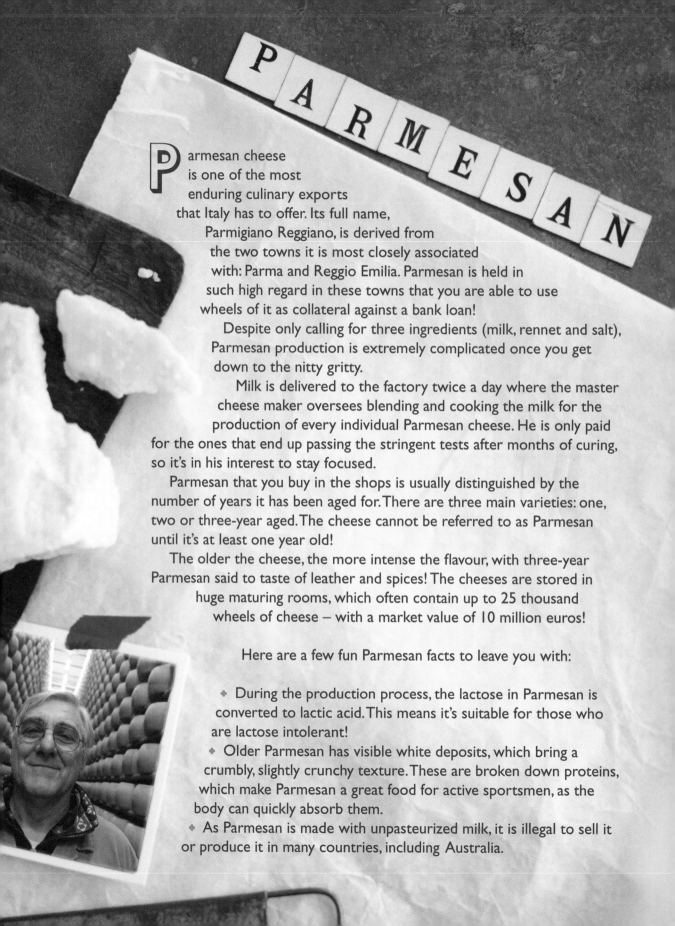

This is focaccia, Jim, but not as we know it. Recco is a small coastal town famous for this amazing pastry and cheese creation, which is completely different to the focaccia bread you find in the UK. We were shown how to make this recipe by twin brothers in their seventies. Encouragingly for us, they have run a restaurant together for 40 years and still haven't fallen out.

FOCACCIA DI RECCO
LIGURIA

300g '00' flour
25ml olive oil, plus extra
   for drizzling
½ teaspoon sea salt, plus
   extra for for sprinkling
250g stracchino cheese (also
   known as crescenza, or a
   mild fontina or taleggio)

Preheat the oven to 250°C/230°C fan/Gas 9.

Pour the flour into a mound on a clean work surface and make a well in the middle with your hand.

Pour in 150ml water, the olive oil and salt and begin to bring in the sides to incorporate the flour. As it starts to become a dough, pull in the remaining flour. Knead the dough well for 10 minutes until you have a smooth and elastic consistency.

Cut the dough in half, form into balls, cover with cling film and rest at room temperature for half an hour.

Roll out one of the balls into a disc the thickness of two pound coins. Then (this is the tricky bit) pick up the dough and rest it on the backs of your hands at the 10 and 2 position. Stretch the dough between your hands and keep the dough moving around (like turning a car steering wheel). The dough should be quite forgiving, but be careful not to stretch the middle too much.

Continued...

Lay the bottom layer over a large baking sheet, stretching the dough over the edges of the pan to get it as thin as possible. Dot the dough with dollops of the cheese.

Stretch out the other dough ball and place on top of the cheese, again stretching the dough over the edges.

Esnsure the dough is sealed at the edges and trim off the excess. Rip small holes in the top dough layer to let the steam out.

Drizzle with a little extra olive oil and a pinch of salt and bake in the oven for 10 minutes until the cheese has melted and the dough is golden brown.

Serve the focaccia on its own with a cold beer – definitely not one for the health conscious.

Farinata is not really a pizza at all – it slipped into the pizza section of this book because it's inherently flat and round. Made from chickpea flour, it's essentially an Italian take on Yorkshire pudding, eaten on its own straight out of the oven. We tried farinata in a town called Savona. In the town square they have a large war memorial, and every evening at 6pm a bell rings out and at that moment, for a full minute, every person in the square stops and turns to face the statue. We are talking about hundreds of people. It was an incredible sight.

FARINATA (CHICKPEA FLATBREAD)

LIGURIA

250g chickpea flour
1 teaspoon sea salt
50ml extra virgin olive oil
Sprig of rosemary leaves,
    finely chopped
2 tablespoons olive oil
Sea salt

In a bowl, whisk together the chickpea flour, salt, extra virgin olive oil and rosemary leaves with 250ml water until you have a smooth batter. Leave to rest for 20 minutes.

Preheat the oven to 220°C/200°C fan/Gas 7.

Heat the olive oil on the hob in a large ovenproof frying pan (or we've found that our old paella dish does the job really well). Swirl it round to make sure the whole pan is oiled.

Ladle in the batter, about ¾cm deep, and turn down the heat slightly. Cook for a minute or so before transferring to the oven.

Cook, without turning, for 10–15 minutes until golden brown and completely set.

Leave to cool slightly, rip into pieces and sprinkle with sea salt.

This is a brilliant way to use up some of the excess pizza dough you might have left over and is simple enough to pull together in even the most hungover state. The only decision you have to make is whether you go for red or brown sauce.

Sourdough bacon butties

LONDON

SERVES 4

1 x ball of Neapolitan Pizza Dough (see recipe on page 80)
3–4 slices of pancetta (depending on how hungry or hungover you are)
Olive oil
Red or brown sauce

Preheat the oven to 200°C/180°C fan/Gas 6. Take the dough ball and put it on a baking tray. Bake the dough ball for 10–12 minutes until it has browned nicely and has a hollow sound when you tap the bottom of it with your finger.

Fry the pancetta on a medium heat until crispy.

Cut open your bun and drizzle with olive oil. Add the pancetta and your choice of sauce. Then sit/lie down and enjoy!

MAINS

One of the most fascinating things we witnessed during our pilgrimage was how the food in Italy changes geographically. The food in the South is very different to that in the North and is affected by two key factors – the temperature and the amount of money people have. As you head north, you can feel the food getting richer and using more expensive ingredients like cream, truffles, hams and cheeses in abundance (and the waistlines tend to grow in proportion – Milan excluded!).

As you can see from the recipes that follow, our hearts lie with 'cucina povera' – recipes created with simpler ingredients from the southern regions of Calabria and Campania. We've thrown in some of the heavy-hitting Tuscan dishes for those colder winter nights when you need something really filling!

Ragù is a Neapolitan institution. If you walk down the back streets of Naples on a Sunday, you can smell the ragù wafting out of every window. It differs from its Bolognese cousin as it's made from whole cuts of meat, not mince, and it's also a two-course affair. You eat the tomato sauce first with pasta and then the meat with greens for secondo. It's a classic example of cucina povera, making what you have go a really long way!

The Neapolitan Ragù Sunday Dinner

SERVES 4

CAMPANIA

Olive oil
500g beef brisket
500g pork spare ribs
200g Italian sausages
4 slices of pancetta
1 onion, diced
1 celery stalk, diced
1 carrot, diced
2 tablespoons tomato purée
1 wine glass of water (or red wine if you're feeling fancy)
3 tins of San Marzano (or any good-quality Italian) tomatoes
2 bay leaves
Sea salt and black pepper
Handful of basil leaves
Pasta and good bread, to serve
Friarielli (see Salsicce e Friarielli recipe on page 92) or your favourite green vegetables: kale, broccoli, green beans, spring greens etc...

Heat the olive oil in a large heavy-bottom pot and brown all of your meat. Try not to overcrowd the pan – you many need to do it in batches. Set aside.

In the same pan, sweat your pancetta, onion, celery and carrot for a few minutes before stirring in the tomato purée to cook through for a couple more minutes.

Deglaze the pan with the glass of water or wine and use a wooden spoon to get all the caramelized bits off the bottom of the pan (that's all good flavour!)

Add in the tomatoes and the bay leaves and return the meat to the pot (including all the juices that have collected).

Bring to the boil and then turn down the heat to a REALLY gentle simmer – we're talking one bubble every 10 seconds or so.

Cover with a lid and cook for around 2 hours (stirring every now and then to make sure the sauce isn't catching), or until the meat is falling off the bone and the sauce is thick and rich. Season to taste and add the basil.

Pull the meat back out and and set aside.

Serve the sauce with your favourite pasta, followed by the meat piled up in a big dish with your favourite green vegetables and some good bread.

This is the port city of Livorno's spin on a fish stew found up and down the west coast. Although there are probably more cruise liners in its port than fishing trawlers these days, there is still a fishing community here. They've made this stew for hundreds of years using 'pesce povero' or 'poor fish' – the fish that you cannot easily sell. You can use any seafood in season, the only important thing to remember is that you need five varieties, one for each 'C' in the name. God, we love Italians!

CACCIUCCO
(FISH SOUP/STEW)

SERVES 4

TUSCANY

500g mussels and/or clams
Olive oil
1 onion, diced
1 celery stalk, diced
1 carrot, diced
2 cloves of garlic, finely
   chopped
Good pinch of peperoncino
   (dried chilli flakes)
1 bay leaf
Sprig of thyme
1 glass of red wine
2 tablespoons red
   wine vinegar
2 tins of San Marzano (or
   any good-quality Italian)
   tomatoes, chopped
500ml fish stock or water
1kg white fish fillets (anything
   you like, maybe sole, mullet,
   monkfish, gurnard, eel,
   hake, John Dory etc.), cut
   into bite-sized chunks
500g cleaned squid or
   octopus
8 slices of good bread,
   toasted and rubbed with a
   clove of garlic, to serve
Sea salt and black pepper
Handful of chopped parsley

First, clean your mussels and/or clams by scrubbing them under cold water, discarding any that are broken or open already and don't close when tapped. Scrape away any barnacles from the mussels and remove the beards. Leave the clams for a couple of hours in clean water to get rid of any grit.

Heat a little olive oil in a large soup pan and gently fry the onion, celery, carrot and garlic for 5 minutes until softened.

Add the peperoncino, bay leaf and thyme before adding the red wine and vinegar, cooking out the alcohol for a couple of minutes.

Next, add in the tomatoes and the fish stock (water will do).

Allow everything to simmer gently for about 15 minutes, slightly reducing and intensifying the flavours.

Now it's time for the fish: add them in order of how long they take to cook. As a rule, fish fillets, then shellfish, then the squid/octopus, which needs to just lightly poach before it goes rubbery. These should take no longer than 5 minutes in total to cook.

Place the garlic toast in the bottom of a large tureen and pour over the stew. Season, sprinkle over some parsley and serve immediately.

We met Sabato on the outskirts of Naples on the search for San Marzano tomatoes. On the weekends he runs a cookery school and café with his wife in Sarno, a small town that sits on the opposite side of Mount Vesuvius to Naples. By day, however, Sabato is a third-generation artichoke farmer. This double life puts him in a strong position to have an opinion on artichoke risotto and this recipe he showed us is hard to beat!

SABATO'S ARTICHOKE RISOTTO

SERVES 4

CAMPANIA

6 young artichoke hearts or
   3 larger ones (you can also
   use jarred artichoke hearts
   if you can't find fresh)
1.2 litres chicken stock
1 shallot, diced
½ a celery stalk, diced
Olive oil
4 handfuls of Arborio rice
   (1 handful per person)
½ a glass of white wine
Small handful of grated
   Parmesan
2 tablespoons butter
Small handful of chopped
   parsley

To prepare the artichokes, trim and peel the stems, leaving just a few centimetres, and pull away the outer leaves until you get to the more tender yellow centre. Using a serrated knife cut off the top third of the artichoke to expose the choke, which should be scooped out with a teaspoon.

Place the trimmed artichokes in the chicken stock and poach on a low heat as you prepare the rest of the risotto.

In a heavy-bottom saucepan, gently fry the shallot and celery in 3 tablespoons of olive oil for around 5 minutes until soft but with no colour.

Stir in the rice, making sure every grain gets coated in the oil. Toast for about 3 minutes until the edges of the rice grains begin to go translucent.

Pour in the wine and let it reduce down until the pan is dry again.

Next, while constantly stirring, add in the stock, ladle by ladle, allowing the pan to go dry before adding the next. This will help to coax out as much starch as possible from the rice to create a creamy texture.

Once you have incorporated all of the stock, the rice should be tender, but with slight resistance under the tooth.

Stir in the Parmesan, butter and parsley, cover with a lid and leave to rest for 2 minutes.

By this point your artichokes should also be cooked. Slice each heart into wedges and stir into the risotto.

Serve in warmed bowls with extra Parmesan and a drizzle (hate that word, but it's exactly what you need) of olive oil.

Agostino is an extremely smooth individual – all sharp suits and Marlboro reds. To be honest, he wasn't exactly what we'd pictured when we set off to meet the head of the nduja co-operative in Spilinga. I'm sure our sausage producers aren't as dapper! He is extremely proud of his product and having lived in Spilinga all his life, he has picked up a few tips on how to cook with it. After a day at the nduja factory, we went back to his and he made us this dish – probably the simplest pasta sauce you are ever likely to find.

AGOSTINO'S NDUJA FUSILLI

CALABRIA

400g dried fusilli
Olive oil
2 cloves of garlic, finely sliced
1 tablespoon finely chopped
  parsley stalks
2 heaped teaspoons nduja
Small handful of parsley
  leaves, chopped
Grated Parmesan

The first thing to do is to get your pasta cooking as the sauce is ready in a fraction of the time.

In a saucepan, bring a little olive oil, the garlic and parsley stalks up to a medium heat and fry gently until the garlic begins to take colour.

Stir in the nduja, which will immediately begin to soften, releasing all the spicy, bright red oils.

Keep the sauce on a gentle heat for a few minutes so that the meat fries in its own fat and caramelizes, bringing out the sweetness.

Drain your pasta and toss with the sauce and the parsley leaves.

Serve in warmed bowls with a grating of Parmesan.

Nduja is one of our favourite discoveries from the pilgrimage – a seriously spicy sausage that packs a punch.

It is made from the fattiest and tastiest parts of the pig, the cheeks and the belly, and these cuts also give it a unique quality – it is spreadable (almost part sausage, part pâté).

In the south of Italy, people eat it on toast. That is braver than it sounds as the other key ingredient in nduja is Calabrian chillies. Some recipes call for up to 50 per cent of the content of the sausage to be chilli! Once everything has been minced together, the mixture is encased in a pig's intestine, smoked and then cured for 3 months. All in all, it is not for the faint-hearted.

Nduja is a product of its surroundings. The town of Spilinga is located in the heart of Calabria, the region of Italy most famous for, shall we say, operating a 'favour-based' economy. We certainly ended up at one or two lunches where no money changed hands!

The people of Spilinga are proud of their local product and it's certainly starting to make more regular appearances on restaurant menus across the UK. It's a versatile ingredient, adding an incredible meaty, spicy flavour to any number of dishes. And, most importantly, it's brilliant on pizzas, melting into the topping and oozing distinctive and delicious red oils. One tip though: do not spend 48 hours living solely on nduja like we did in Calabria. Make sure you eat your greens as well!

You can buy nduja at many Italian delis and also at www.natoora.co.uk. Check out the recipe for Nduja Fusilli opposite – it's all about pasta sauce that takes less time to cook than the pasta itself!

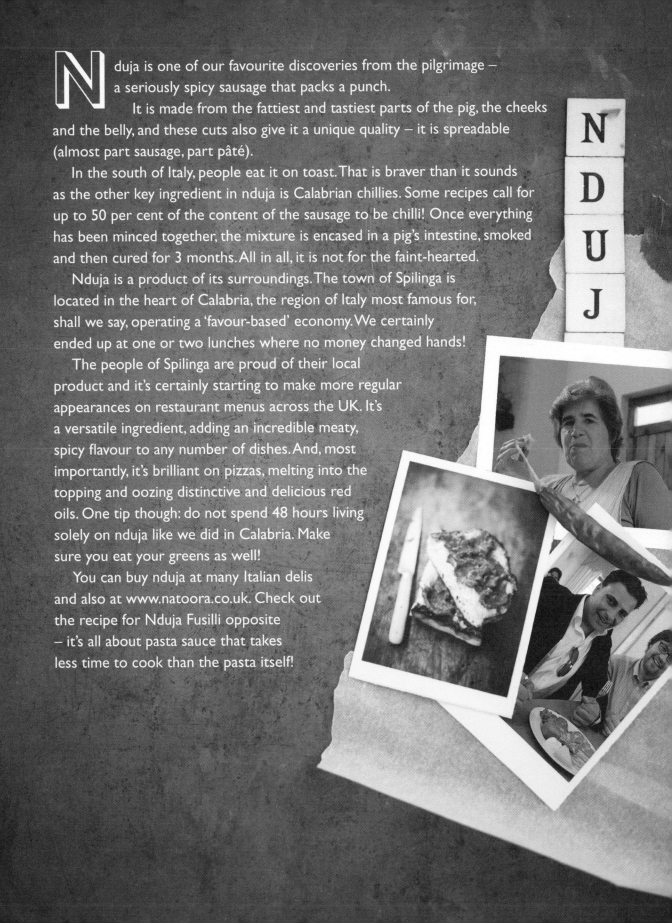

This is a classic Neapolitan dish and is certainly not one for those counting calories (unless they are really good at counting). Fried aubergine, mozzarella, Parmesan, tomato and olive oil – it's the ideal winter dish and the perfect alternative to lasagne.

Parmigiana di melanzane
(Aubergine Parmigiana)

SERVES 4–6

CAMPANIA

3 large aubergines
Olive oil
Sea salt and black pepper
1 onion, finely chopped
1 clove of garlic, finely chopped
1 celery stalk, finely chopped
2 tins of San Marzano (or any good-quality Italian) tomatoes, chopped
1 tablespoon red wine vinegar
Pinch of caster sugar
Handful of basil leaves
2 good handfuls of grated Parmesan
125g ball of buffalo mozzarella, torn into bite-sized pieces

First up, preheat your oven to 200°C/180°C fan/Gas 6.

Top and tail your aubergines, leaving the skins on (purists wouldn't, but life's too short). Slice into pieces the thickness of two pound coins.

You can fry the aubergines, but we prefer the charred flavour of barbecuing or griddling them. Brush the slices with olive oil, season with salt and pepper and grill until they have softened and taken on a good colour. Set them aside.

In a large saucepan, gently fry the onion, garlic and celery in a couple of tablespoons of olive oil for about 10 minutes until they're sweet and softened.

Add in the tomatoes and red wine vinegar and simmer for about 10 minutes to cook out the tomatoes.

Season with salt, pepper and a pinch of sugar to balance out the vinegar. Take off the heat and stir in the basil.

Now it's time to assemble. Spread a thin layer of the tomato sauce over the bottom of a large gratin dish, top with a pinch of Parmesan, a couple of pieces of mozzarella, a twist of pepper and then a layer of the aubergines.

Repeat this process until the dish is full or you've run out of ingredients (or both if you've judged it right!). Finish with a little sauce, Parmesan, the rest of the mozzarella and a trickle of good olive oil.

Bake in the oven for about 30 minutes until the top has gone golden brown and the tomatoes are bubbling up the sides of the dish.

It's great eaten straight away with good bread and a simple green salad, but it can also be eaten cold – most likely straight from the fridge at about 2am!

Some foods are never going to be suitable for a first date – and this is certainly one of them (that black-tinged smile only a mother could love). To be honest, though, if you can't woo someone by cooking them this awesome risotto, then it's just not meant to be.

RISOTTO NERO (SQUID INK RISOTTO) WITH PAN-FRIED GARLIC SQUID

SERVES 4

VENETO

1.2 litres light fish stock
  or water
1 shallot, diced
½ a celery stalk, diced
Olive oil
4 handfuls of Arborio rice
  (1 handful per person)
½ a glass of white wine
2 tablespoons butter
2 x 4g sachets of squid ink
  (available in most delis,
  fishmongers and some
  supermarkets)
2 small fresh squid, cleaned
  (get your fishmonger to do
  this for you), about 300g
  once prepped
1 large clove of garlic,
  chopped

Put the stock on a low heat.

In a heavy-bottom saucepan, gently fry the shallot and celery in 3 tablespoons of olive oil for around 5 minutes until soft but with no colour.

Stir in the rice, ensuring every grain gets coated in the oil. Toast for about 3 minutes until the edges of the rice grains begin to go translucent.

Pour in the wine and let it reduce down until the pan is dry again.

Next, while constantly stirring, add in the stock, ladle by ladle, allowing the pan to go dry before adding the next. This will help to coax out as much starch as possible from the rice to create a creamy texture.

Once you have incorporated all of the stock, the rice should be tender and soft, but with slight resistance under the tooth. Stir in the butter, cover with a lid and leave to rest for 2 minutes.

Stir in the squid ink – it's incredible how such a small amount will turn the whole risotto jet black!

To prepare the squid, take the body and run your knife up the inside so it opens out like a book. Then cut down the middle so you have two halves. Next, take each piece and gently score a crisscross pattern with a dinner knife on one side. For the tentacles, simply cut them in half.

Heat a couple of tablespoons of olive oil in a frying pan and add the garlic. Just as the garlic begins to colour, add the squid and quickly fry for 1–2 minutes. Make sure you don't overcook the squid as it will go tough!

Serve the risotto in a big bowl with the squid sitting pretty on top.

Telline clams (pronounced tell-een-eh) are found off the Lazio coast. We spent an afternoon dredging for them in the surf (and then another few hours trying to drive Concetta back off the beach – three wheels and sand do NOT mix). They are delicious served as simply as possible, letting their delicate flavour speak for itself. You should be able to get them from most good fishmongers, no dredging required. If not, small 'vongole' clams are a good substitute.

TELLINE CLAM LINGUINE

SERVES 4

LAZIO

600g telline clams
400g dried linguine
Olive oil
2 cloves of garlic, finely chopped
Good pinch of peperoncino (dried chilli flakes)
1 tablespoon finely sliced parsley stalks
Sea salt and black pepper
Handful of chopped parsley

First, clean your clams by scrubbing under cold water, discarding any that are broken or open already and don't close when tapped. Leave the clams for a couple of hours in clean water to get rid of any grit.

When you're ready to eat, cook your linguine in a large pot of boiling salted water for about a minute less than the packet instructions (to keep it 'al dente').

At the same time, heat 3 tablespoons of olive oil in a large frying pan with a lid and gently fry the garlic, peperoncino and parsley stalks for about 30 seconds before throwing in the clams.

Cover the pan with the lid to steam the clams for a minute or two until all of the shells have opened.

Spoon a little of the pasta water into the sauce to help create a good consistency. Drain the cooked pasta and add it to the sauce.

Check for seasoning and finish with a handful of parsley.

The best soups in our view are the ones that dance the line between soup and stew, and this Tuscan classic definitely qualifies. 'Ribollita' means 're-boiled', and was traditionally a way for Tuscan peasants to use up cheap vegetables and stale bread by adding it to yesterday's minestrone. It was created to fill you up so it should be a thick, gutsy soup that doesn't hold back on flavour. So if you want to add more garlic, chilli or whatever you fancy, go for it!

Ribollita
(Tuscan bread soup)

TUSCANY

SERVES 4

2 onions, diced
2 carrots, diced
2 celery stalks, diced
3 cloves of garlic, crushed
Pinch of peperoncino (dried chilli flakes)
2 bay leaves
3 tablespoons olive oil
1 tin of San Marzano (or any good-quality Italian) tomatoes, chopped
1 tin of cannellini beans, rinsed and drained
Rind of a piece of Parmesan (optional)
2 good handfuls of stale sourdough bread, torn into chunks
3 big handfuls of shredded cavolo nero (Savoy cabbage or kale are also good)
Sea salt and black pepper
Good-quality extra virgin olive oil

In a saucepan, gently fry the onion, carrot, celery, garlic, chilli flakes and bay leaves in the 3 tablespoons of olive oil for about 20 minutes until the vegetables have softened and they've taken on a little colour.

Stir in the tomatoes, beans, Parmesan rind and 500ml water, then leave to simmer for half an hour, covered with a lid.

Throw in your bread and cavolo nero and simmer for a further 10 minutes. Season with salt and pepper to taste.

Serve in bowls with a trickle of really good-quality extra virgin olive oil.

This soup really benefits from being left overnight to let all the flavours marry together.

After a day acting like complete tourists in Pisa (photos holding up the leaning tower etc.), we stopped off at a little trattoria in the main square and ordered this pasta dish. Tuscan butternut squash, when it's in season, is so sweet, and near perfection paired with the salty, smoky pancetta. We followed this perfect day out by getting arrested for driving the Ape the wrong way down a one-way street. Smooth…

PANCETTA AND SQUASH PAPPARDELLE

SERVES 4

TUSCANY

200g pancetta, roughly chopped
1 leek, roughly chopped
½ a glass of white wine
300g butternut squash flesh, roughly chopped
400g dried pappardelle
Olive oil
Sea salt and black pepper
Handful of grated Parmesan

In a large saucepan, fry the pancetta and the leek over a medium heat until the pancetta has browned slightly and the leek has softened.

Deglaze the pan with the white wine, and then add the squash.

Cover the pan with a lid and cook slowly for about half an hour until the squash has cooked down and taken on an amazing sweetness.

Cook your pasta in a large pot of boiling salted water, before draining and tossing in the sauce with a good glug of olive oil. Again, if you need to, you can add some of the pasta water to help create a good sauce. Season well.

Turn out into a big serving bowl and finish with grated Parmesan.

This is an absolute Roman staple and probably the simplest recipe in the book. With just four ingredients (well, five if you include water...), it's hard to believe that you can really go wrong. But in the eyes of a Roman, if it's not done right, they're not eating it! We arrived in Rome a little 'light of pocket' (thanks to our incredible but cripplingly expensive time on the Amalfi Coast!) and met up with some students who took us out for this cheap eat. And we're so glad we did...

CACIO E PEPE
(CHEESE AND PEPPER SPAGHETTI)

SERVES 4

LAZIO

500g dried spaghetti
2 tablespoons butter
1 teaspoon freshly cracked black pepper
4 heaped tablespoons good-quality grated pecorino (you can use Parmesan, but we do recommend trying to get your hands on this sharper Roman alternative made from sheep's milk)

Cook the spaghetti in a large pot with about half the salted water you normally would, and for 1 minute less than the packet instructions suggest (to get an 'al dente' pasta).

Drain the pasta, reserving about 125ml of the starchy water.

In a large frying pan, melt half the butter and add the pepper. Gently fry until the butter stops foaming, then add the reserved water and boil for about a minute. This helps to extract the pepper flavour.

Add the remaining butter and three-quarters of the cheese, then toss the spaghetti in the sauce until it all emulsifies and coats the spaghetti.

Serve at the table in a big bowl with the rest of the pecorino sprinkled on top and an extra twist of pepper.

POLENTA

Polenta is a strange one. It's absolutely everywhere in Italy and one of the ingredients you can expect to find in every kitchen cupboard. More than that, it exists in some form in almost every continent in the world. Only the Brits seem to have shunned it, although given its similarity in consistency to 'gruel', Charles Dickens and the Victorians gave it a pretty bad name before people even got to try it!

Made from ground maize (corn), polenta is hugely versatile. It is initially boiled in water, then laced with Parmesan and butter to create a creamy, mashed-potato-like dish. This is delicious on its own, but can also be grilled, fried into chips or baked into a pie. If you ever visit Tuscany, you need to be prepared to try it in all its forms – they really can't get enough of it.

We spent a fantastic autumn afternoon in the town of Sassetta, where they hold an annual food festival and donkey race. The streets were lined with hundreds of producers and traders all pushing their wares. And polenta was everywhere, with seemingly every stall offering regional polenta delights.

The highlight was one of the simpler variants: creamed polenta served with wild boar sausages in red wine (see our version of the recipe on page 150).

This is basically the Italian version of sausage and mash. In Tuscany, the polenta itself is served from huge vats, proper witches' cauldron stuff, and attentively watched at all times by a man who clearly takes polenta very seriously. And he has every right to – accompanied by red wine in a plastic cup it was one of the most delicious dishes we tried on our whole trip. Maybe this street food thing will catch on...

BUTTERED POLENTA SERVED WITH WILD BOAR SAUSAGES IN RED WINE

SERVES 4

TUSCANY

For the sausages in red wine
8 good-sized wild boar sausages
Olive oil
4 slices of pancetta, chopped
2 large cloves of garlic, finely chopped
1 onion, sliced
⅓ of a bottle of good red wine
285ml chicken stock
A sprig of rosemary
1 bay leaf
6 juniper berries, crushed
1 tablespoon softened butter
1 teaspoon plain flour

For the polenta
500g polenta
3 good handfuls of grated Parmesan
100g butter
Sea salt and black pepper

In a heavy-bottom casserole dish, fry the sausages in a couple of tablespoons of olive oil until they're browned all over. Lift the sausages out of the pan and set aside.

In the same pan, gently fry the pancetta, garlic and onion for 10–15 minutes until soft and sweet.

Use the red wine to deglaze the bottom of the pan and boil hard for a minute or so to cook off the alcohol.

Pour in the chicken stock and add the rosemary, bay leaf and crushed juniper berries.

Return the sausages to the pan and gently simmer with the lid on for 30 minutes.

At the same time, bring 2 litres of water to the boil and whisk in the polenta. Keep whisking until you have a smooth consistency.

Turn down the heat and VERY gently simmer the polenta, stirring regularly, with the lid ajar for about an hour. If it begins to catch on the bottom, then add a little more water. You are looking for a thick, porridge-like consistency.

Remove the sausages from the sauce and set aside. Mix the softened butter with the flour and stir through the sauce. Simmer for a further 5 minutes until it has thickened and turned glossy. Return the sausages to the pan and take off the heat to rest with the lid on.

The polenta should now have a fantastic texture, but it needs flavour!

Take off the heat and stir through the Parmesan and butter and season well. Leave to rest with the lid on for a couple of minutes.

To serve, pour the polenta onto a large platter and make a well in the middle. Pour the sausages and sauce into the well and drizzle with olive oil.

No one knows why it's called 'whore's spaghetti', but we are guessing this would be the perfect dish for a busy working girl that didn't have time to go to the shops, so pulled together dishes from things she had in the cupboard. This isn't a subtle sauce and should be an assault on the senses, with the saltiness from the anchovies, sharpness from the capers, sweetness from the tomatoes and a good punch of spice from the chilli.

SPAGHETTI ALLA PUTTANESCA
(WHORE'S SPAGHETTI)

SERVES 4

CAMPANIA

2 cloves of garlic, finely sliced
Good pinch of peperoncino (dried chilli flakes)
8 anchovy fillets, chopped
Olive oil
2 tins of San Marzano (or any good-quality Italian) tomatoes, chopped
400g dried spaghetti
Handful of pitted black olives
Small handful of capers
Sea salt and black pepper (if needed)

In a saucepan, gently fry the garlic, peperoncino and chopped anchovies in 3 tablespoons of olive oil until the anchovies have melted and the garlic has taken on a slight colour.

Add the tomatoes to the pan and simmer gently for about 15 minutes until you have a rich sauce.

At the same time, boil your spaghetti in a large pot of boiling, salted water for about a minute less than the packet instructions (to get an 'al dente' pasta).

Once the sauce is ready, stir in the olives and capers.

Check for seasoning and then toss with the drained pasta.

We stopped off for the afternoon in the picture perfect Tuscan town of Montepulciano – world-renowned for its red wine production and famously the setting for the *Twilight* films. Obviously enthralled by both, we decided to focus on the wine. There was a biblical rainstorm while we were there, so we spent most of the time in the huge wine cellars tasting different wines... Tough gig. This recipe makes great use of the local wine and was the ultimate antidote to the weather.

TUSCAN HUNTSMAN'S CHICKEN WITH GREEN OLIVES

SERVES 4

TUSCANY

8 chicken thighs and legs (and maybe a couple of wings for good measure)

500ml good red wine (but not that good!)

4 cloves of garlic, minced

4 bay leaves

Flour, for dusting

Olive oil

4 anchovy fillets, minced

1 heaped tablespoon tomato purée

500ml chicken stock

Sea salt and black pepper

Good handful of stoned green olives

Good bread or Buttered Polenta (see recipe page 150), to serve

Put the chicken in a large bowl, pour in the red wine and add the garlic and bay leaves. Leave to marinate in the fridge for at least 2 hours, but best overnight.

Drain the chicken, reserving the wine, and roll the pieces in flour.

In a large casserole dish, brown the meat in a couple of tablespoons of olive oil. Try not to overcrowd the pan – you may need to do it in two batches. Set the meat aside.

Put the same pan back on the heat and fry the anchovies in a little olive oil until they dissolve.

Stir in the tomato purée and cook for about a minute before adding the chicken stock.

Return the chicken to the pan and cook on a low heat for about 30–40 minutes until the chicken is 'falling off the bone'. Check for seasoning.

Throw in the olives and serve with good bread or buttered polenta.

You must have faith with this dish. Once you have finished cooking it, having followed the instructions below word for word, you will no doubt feel a hint of disappointment. There's no avoiding the fact that this one is not a looker. Curdled milk can be offputting, but you must soldier on – never judge a book by its cover and all that. Cooking in milk gives the meat much more flavour and if the look really bothers you, just eat it with your eyes closed. Or in the dark.

SHOULDER OF PORK COOKED IN MILK WITH SAGE

SERVES 4–6

EMILIA-ROMAGNA

Shoulder of pork, rolled and tied (get your butcher to do this), about 2kg
Olive oil
2 tablespoons butter
4 large cloves of garlic
Small handful of sage leaves
3 bay leaves
1 litre whole milk

In a large, heavy-bottom pan, brown the pork in a couple of tablespoons of olive oil.

Pull out the meat and set aside.

Melt the butter in the same pan and gently fry the garlic, sage and bay leaves on a low heat for a couple of minutes.

Pour in the milk and bring to the boil.

Return the pork to the pan and cook on the lowest heat possible, covered with the lid slightly ajar, for at least 2 hours until the meat is tender.

Allow the meat to rest for 10 minutes before slicing thinly and serving with the split sauce, mashed potatoes and your favourite greens.

We were served this dish in a small beachside fish restaurant in Calabria after we had spent the morning tasting chilli with a peperoncino farmer called Giuseppe. Our mouths were still on fire from trying to out-do each other on the Scoville scale, and we really could not taste the sea bass at all (we were just glad it wasn't served with chilli). We had to try the dish again once we got home to really appreciate how delicious it is!

Sea bass with bay, orange and braised fennel

SERVES 2–4

CALABRIA

3 fennel bulbs
Grated zest of 1 orange
½ teaspoon fennel seeds
Olive oil
½ a glass of white wine
Sea salt and black pepper
4 small sea bass (about 300g each) or 2 larger (about 500g each), gutted and descaled
4 bay leaves
Small handful of chopped parsley

Cut off the tops and the stems of the fennel bulbs and remove the tough outer layer. Set the fennel tops aside and throw the stems away. Halve the fennel bulbs, and then cut each half into 6 wedges.

Place the fennel in a large roasting tin with the orange zest, fennel seeds, 2 tablespoons of olive oil, the wine and a pinch of salt and pepper. Mix everything together well.

Cover with foil and roast for 20 minutes.

Season your fish, inside and out, with salt and pepper.

Stuff the cavities of the fish with the fennel tops and the bay leaves.

Lay the fish on top of the part-roasted fennel bulbs and return to the oven for 20–25 minutes until the flesh is opaque and juicy and the fennel is tender.

Serve at the table with a sprinkling of parsley, new potatoes or any potatoes you fancy come to think of it...

Smoked scamorza is a cow's milk cheese from Puglia and, at first glance, it's not much to look at. The way it's tied with string and then hung up to dry makes it look a little like a fat person being strangled! However, the smoked variety has a deep and nutty flavour that, not to put too fine a point on it, is one of the most delicious things in the whole world. This is not a 'quick supper', it's a dish you should really take your time over and not overcomplicate with hundreds of ingredients.

Smoked Scamorza, Chicken and Pancetta Tortellini in Chicken Broth

Serves 4

PUGLIA

100g pancetta, finely chopped
1 raw chicken breast, skinned
1 egg
25–50ml double cream
1 tablespoon breadcrumbs
Black pepper
125g smoked scamorza, finely diced
1 batch of the basic Fresh Pasta recipe (see page 52)
1 litre good-quality chicken stock
Good-quality extra virgin olive oil

Fry the pancetta until golden brown, drain on kitchen paper and leave to cool.

In a food processor, combine the chicken breast, egg, cream, breadcrumbs and a good pinch of pepper. Use the pulse setting as you don't want to overwork the mixture.

Transfer the mixture to a mixing bowl and use a wooden spoon to combine with the pancetta and scamorza.

Roll the pasta out thinly (about the thickness of five sheets of paper) and then cut into squares, each about the size of a Post-it note.

Take a teaspoon of the mixture and place it in the middle of each square.

Dab the edges of each pasta square with water to help it seal, then fold the square in half to make a triangle, with the mixture in the middle.

Press to seal the edges, ensuring there are no air bubbles as they'll explode when you cook them.

Next, fold the triangle where the filling ends to make what looks like a boat shape.

Then, take the two opposite corners and wrap them around the tip of your little finger, pinching to seal.

Bring the stock to the boil and add the tortellini.

Cook for 2–3 minutes until the pasta is tender and the scamorza inside is melted and stringy.

Serve in big bowls with a trickle of good olive oil and a few cracks of black pepper.

Lamb is a surprisingly rare find in Italy, where the pig is the undisputed meat king. Lamb is, however, reserved for the real family celebrations and is a regular on the Italian Christmas dinner table (and I think we can all agree is a much better choice than turkey). This is a delicious way of serving lamb: the saltiness of the anchovies complements the sweetness of the meat brilliantly and the potatoes take on all the flavours of the dish. A great twist on a classic English roast.

ROAST LEG OF LAMB WITH ANCHOVIES AND OREGANO

SERVES 4–6

ACROSS ITALY

50g tin of anchovies, chopped
4 cloves of garlic, crushed
Small bunch of fresh oregano
Juice of 1 lemon
Leg of lamb, about 1.5–2kg
   (bone in)
8 roasting potatoes (eg
   Russet or Maris Piper),
   peeled and quartered
Olive oil
Sea salt

In a bowl, combine the chopped anchovies, garlic, oregano leaves, lemon juice and the oil from the anchovy tin into a paste.

Place the lamb in a large roasting tin, spread all over with the paste and allow to marinate in the fridge for at least 2 hours, but overnight is better.

Take the lamb out of the fridge and allow the meat to come back to room temperature.

Get the lamb in the oven on full whack (around 250°C/230°C fan/ Gas 9) to brown for 10 minutes before turning it down to 200°C/ 180°C fan/Gas 6.

Coat the potatoes with olive oil and a good pinch of sea salt, then add to the tin. Roast for an hour until the lamb is pink in the middle and the potatoes are golden brown and crisp.

Allow the lamb to rest for 20 minutes before carving.

Rabbit features heavily in Tuscan cooking and seems insanely overlooked in Britain given how many wild rabbits we have. Thumper from *Bambi* might be partly to blame for that. Rabbit can also be hard to cook without becoming dry, which is why it's absolutely perfect for stews or a ragù. This recipe brings a delicious gamey flavour to your standard beef or pork ragù.

BRAISED RABBIT RAGÙ WITH PAPPARDELLE

SERVES 4

TUSCANY

1kg rabbit, jointed (get your butcher to do this)
Olive oil
1 onion, diced
1 carrot, diced
1 celery stalk, diced
2 cloves of garlic, crushed
2 bay leaves
1 teaspoon thyme leaves
1 glass of white wine
2 tins of San Marzano (or any good-quality Italian) tomatoes
500ml chicken stock
Sea salt and black pepper
Small handful of chopped parsley
400g cooked pappardelle, to serve
Grated Parmesan, to serve

Brown the rabbit pieces in a little olive oil in a large casserole dish.

Set the meat aside and, in the same pan, gently fry the onion, carrot, celery, garlic, bay leaves and thyme for about 15 minutes until the vegetables have softened but not coloured.

Deglaze the pan with the white wine, ensuring you scrape the caramelized bits off the bottom.

Pour in your tomatoes and stock and bring to the boil.

Return the meat to the pan and reduce the heat to a gentle simmer. Cook with the lid ajar on a low heat for around 2 hours until the meat is falling off the bone.

Fish out the meat and set aside until it's cool enough to handle. In the meantime, bring the sauce up to a rapid boil and reduce for about 10–15 minutes until you have a rich, thick sauce.

Once cooled, shred the meat off the bone and return to the sauce. Season to taste and stir through the parsley once the sauce is off the heat.

This ragù is classically served with pappardelle and grated Parmesan.

This dish is served in almost every restaurant in Florence and is the Holy Grail for the meat eater. It's basically just a big T-bone steak, but it's all about the quality of the meat and how you cook it. In Florence they chargrill it over a wood fire. We recommend doing it on the BBQ. It doesn't matter if it's mid-January and snowing outside, fire up the BBQ, put on another jumper and get out there. It's worth it!

Bistecca alla Fiorentina
(T—bone steak with lemon)

SERVES 2 CARNIVORES OR 4 NORMAL PEOPLE

TUSCANY

A T-bone steak, about 1kg, with the bone in (get your butcher to prepare this for you)
Olive oil
Sea salt and black pepper
1 lemon
1 clove of garlic, finely chopped
1 tin of cannellini beans
Small handful of parsley
Rocket salad, to serve

Brush the steak with olive oil and season generously with salt and pepper.

Place your steak on the hot BBQ bars (or, failing that, a screaming hot heavy-duty griddle on the hob) and cook for 2–3 minutes until you have some good bar marks.

Turn the steak and cook for a further 2–3 minutes until you have the matching bar marks on the other side.

Now you need to repeat the process and turn the steak 90 degrees on both sides so that you get the classic 'crisscross' marks on the meat (this is obviously essential!). For a rare steak, you're looking at 12–14 minutes cooking. For medium, 18–20 minutes.

Take the steak off the heat, squeeze over the lemon juice and leave to rest for 10 minutes.

In that time, gently fry the garlic in 2 tablespoons of olive oil until it begins to take on some colour, then add the cannellini beans.

Sauté for a couple of minutes until the beans are warmed through.

Take off the heat before stirring in the parsley and a little squeeze of lemon juice.

Carve the steak at the table and serve with the beans and a fresh rocket salad.

Bollito misto is a dish from the Piedmont region, made up of a variety of meats cooked in stock with vegetables. There's no way round it, boiled meats just don't sound that appealing, but cooked low and slow in a really tasty broth the result is delicate and up there with the best comfort foods. This is our version with a whole chicken, sausages and a good selection of veg (so we can make sure you are getting your five-a-day).

Bollito misto
(pot—boiled chicken dinner)

SERVES 4—6

PIEDMONT

I whole chicken (as good a chicken as you can afford)
I fennel bulb, cut into wedges
2 celery stalks, left whole
I large onion, peeled and studded with cloves
2 carrots, left whole
4 Italian fennel sausages (a good deli should have these or use Cumberland sausages with an added teaspoon of fennel seeds)
2 bay leaves
Sprig of thyme
10 peppercorns
I litre good chicken stock
Sea salt
I batch of Salsa Verde (see our recipe on page 34)
Olive oil

Place your chicken in a snugly fitting, heavy-bottom casserole dish (with a lid).

Pack the vegetables, sausages, herbs and peppercorns around the chicken and pour over the chicken stock. If the stock doesn't completely cover the chicken and vegetables, top up the pan with water.

Season with salt, bring to a gentle simmer and cook with the lid on for 40–50 minutes until the chicken is cooked through.

Take the chicken out of the pan and joint it, removing the legs, breast and wings.

Serve the chicken on a large platter with the sausages, boiled vegetables, some of the stock spooned over the top and our Salsa Verde, and then drizzle over some olive oil.

Caciofiore cheese is unique in a number of ways. It's completely vegetarian as the rennet used to make it is extracted from thistles, not calves' stomachs. It's very old, with a recipe that predates the Roman Empire. And, most impressively, it has a slightly chalky consistency, instantly rendering the expression 'like chalk and cheese' redundant. Daniella and Massimo, the cheese maker, showed us this delicious ravioli recipe – a perfect way to show off the cheese's flavour and consistency.

THE CHEESE MAKER'S WIFE'S CACIOFIORE RAVIOLI

SERVES 4

LAZIO

1 batch of the basic Fresh Pasta recipe (see page 52)

For the filling
2 medium potatoes, peeled, boiled and mashed
250g caciofiore cheese (or taleggio if you can't find it), finely diced into cubes
Small handful of mint leaves
Sea salt and black pepper
Olive oil
2 tablespoons butter
Handful of sage leaves

In a bowl, combine the mashed potato, cheese, mint, a pinch of salt and pepper and 2 tablespoons of olive oil.

Next, roll out your pasta to the thickness of five sheets of paper and cut into two rectangles.

On one sheet, place teaspoons of the filling all over, at 5cm intervals.

Cover with the other sheet of pasta and press to individually seal the ravioli, ensuring you get rid of any air bubbles, as they will explode when cooking.

Now, you can either buy a specific tool for shaping round ravioli or just use something in your kitchen that's the right size and shape (a tumbler works) or cut them out with a knife. If you do use a knife, it's a good idea to crimp the edges of the ravioli with a fork to make sure they stay closed during cooking.

Cook the ravioli in boiling salted water for 3–4 minutes until the pasta is 'al dente' and the cheese has melted.

In a large frying pan, melt the butter and throw in your sage leaves.

Add the ravioli to the pan and fry for a couple of minutes until they're all covered in butter and have taken on a little colour.

Serve in warmed bowls.

Putting a huge meatloaf on the table is the Neapolitan way of saying they like you. It's a real family dish and another great example of the southern Italian style of cooking. It seems strange to us that meatloaf is so big in Italy and the US (it is Homer Simpson's favourite food after doughnuts), but hardly exists in the UK at all. Eat the sauce with pasta as a first course, then eat the meat with your favourite greens and good bread.

PROPER ITALIAN POLPETTONE ALLA NAPOLITANA (NEAPOLITAN MEATLOAF)

SERVES 4

CAMPANIA

2 slices of stale white bread
100ml milk
300g minced beef
200g minced pork
1 large egg
Small handful of grated Parmesan
Handful of pine nuts, lightly toasted in a dry frying pan or under the grill
Sea salt and black pepper
1 small onion, finely diced
2 cloves of garlic, crushed
Olive oil
2 tins of San Marzano (or any good-quality Italian) tomatoes, chopped
Large handful of basil leaves
Pasta, green vegetables and good bread, to serve

Break the stale bread up into a bowl and pour over the milk. Leave to steep for a few minutes.

In a large mixing bowl, combine the meat, bread and milk, egg, Parmesan, pine nuts and a good pinch of salt and pepper. Use your hands to massage all the flavours through the meat. Cover with cling film and chill in the fridge for 20 minutes.

In a large saucepan, gently fry the onion and garlic in 3 tablespoons of olive oil before adding the tomatoes and 100ml water.

Bring to a gentle simmer and cook for 5 minutes. Remove from the heat and then add the basil to the sauce.

Take the meat from the fridge and form into a loaf shape.

Brown the loaf on all sides in a frying pan with olive oil before lowering it into the sauce and cooking in the pan with the lid on for about 15–20 minutes until the meatloaf is cooked through.

Serve the sauce with pasta as a first course before carving the meatloaf and serving as a main course.

PUDDINGS
AND DRINKS

Italian puddings never seem to be treated with the respect they deserve. The French always get the glory. The truth is that Italy has brought the world some of its most enduring creations – ice cream anyone? Lesser known delights like sfogliatelle can also be way tastier than their French equivalents. We have tried to steer clear of dishes you may have heard of, choosing some of the more obscure delights we discovered on our trip.

We have also thrown in a couple of our favourite Italian cocktails for good measure. Aperol Spritz really is the ultimate summer drink, while a Negroni has to be the coolest cocktail going...

———

The unavoidable truth: granita is essentially just a swanky Slush Puppie. However, in place of flavours such as 'blue' or 'red', this recipe calls for the intense aroma of bergamot. With the bitterness of a grapefruit and the sweetness of an orange, this southern Italian citrus fruit is used to make anything from liquors to marmalades. To most of us Brits, bergamots are best known as the key flavour in Earl Grey tea. Try this recipe after a big meal and you'll see that bergamots have so much more to offer.

Lemon and bergamot granita

SERVES 4–6

CALABRIA

200g caster sugar
5 lemons
2 bergamots
200ml whipping cream,
  whipped, to serve

In a saucepan, heat the sugar and 200ml water until the sugar has visibly disappeared, then boil for a couple of minutes, leave to cool and you have a sugar syrup.

Take the pan off the heat and zest the lemons and bergamots, using a vegetable peeler, straight into the syrup. Leave to infuse for 20 minutes.

Juice the lemons and bergamots and add to the syrup.

Sieve the liquid into a stainless-steel bowl and place in the freezer.

Take the bowl out of the freezer every 30–40 minutes and use a fork to break up the ice crystals and whip air into the granita.

Once the granita is firm and has frozen properly, cover with cling film.

To serve, put the granita in the fridge for 20 minutes to soften slightly.

Then, using a granita scraper, if you're fancy enough to have one (or just get at it with a metal spoon), break up the ice crystals. You'll know it is right when it looks like a Slush Puppie!

Serve in a bowl with a dollop of whipped cream and some bergamot zest to decorate.

The people of Naples will only tell you through gritted teeth that it was the French that came up with the rum baba. That doesn't stop every café and bakery in town putting it front and centre of their cake displays. A rum baba consists of a light sponge soaked in a rum sugar syrup. To be clear, there is a reason that rum is the first word in the title of this recipe – make sure you are not driving a car or operating heavy machinery after you have a rum baba with your afternoon tea.

RUM BABA

CAMPANIA

SERVES 2—4

For the batter
25g fresh baker's yeast
50ml milk, at room
   temperature
30g caster sugar
250g plain flour
4 large eggs, beaten
1 teaspoon sea salt
125g room-temperature
   butter

For the syrup
500g caster sugar
100ml dark rum
Apricot jam, for glazing

In a bowl, combine the yeast with the milk and 2 teaspoons of sugar. Leave in a warm place until a foam has formed (about 30 minutes).

In a food mixer (preferably with a dough hook attachment), combine the flour with the eggs and salt.

Once it has come together, add the yeast mixture, butter and the rest of the sugar. Beat until you have a glossy, loose batter.

Butter a large mixing bowl and pour in the batter. Cover with cling film and leave in a warm place until the mixture has doubled in size.

Remove the cling film and 'knock back' the batter by stirring until it returns to its original size.

Ladle the batter into well-buttered ramekins (ovenproof glass tumblers will do fine) until two-thirds full. Leave the batter to rest in the ramekins for 20 minutes. Preheat the oven to 200°C/180°C fan/Gas 6.

Bake in the oven for 20 minutes, the first 10 minutes at 200°C and the second 10 minutes at 180°C/160°C fan/Gas 4.

Heat the sugar and 500ml water in a saucepan until the sugar has visibly disappeared, then boil for a couple of minutes, leave to cool and you have a sugar syrup. Pour in the rum and take off the heat.

When the babas are cooked, turn them out and leave to cool. Prick them all over with a skewer and soak in the hot rum syrup for a couple of minutes.

Heat some apricot jam and glaze the soaked babas.

The babas can be eaten straight up with an extra spoon of syrup poured over them or you can cut them open and fill with whipped cream and fresh fruit.

J

As with all things Neapolitan, there is a huge amount of discussion about how sfogliatelle actually originated – and we highly recommend you never engage a Neapolitan on the subject (Diego Maradona should also be avoided). All you really need to know is that these crunchy creations are the perfect accompaniment to a strong Neapolitan espresso. This is the smooth version called sfogliatelle frolle – just as delicious as its puff pastry cousin, sfogliatelle riccia, but requiring less work.

SFOGLIATELLE FROLLE
(NEAPOLITAN PASTRIES)

CAMPANIA

MAKES 10 PASTRIES

For the dough
100g cold unsalted butter, cubed
200g plain flour
2 egg yolks
50g caster sugar
Pinch of sea salt
Egg glaze made from 1 egg and 1 egg yolk, beaten together

For the filling
80g icing sugar, plus extra for dusting
Vanilla pod, split lengthways with the seeds scraped out
50g semolina
Grated zest of 1 lemon
50g candied peel
Small pinch of sea salt
150g ricotta cheese
1 egg

In a bowl, rub the butter and the flour together until it resembles breadcrumbs.

Next, beat in the egg yolks, sugar, salt and a couple of tablespoons of cold water until you have a stiff dough.

Cover with cling film and rest in the fridge for half an hour.

In a saucepan, heat the sugar, vanilla and 150ml water until the sugar has dissolved. Boil for a couple of minutes, leave to cool and you have a sugar syrup.

Stir in the semolina and cook for 4–5 minutes.

Take the pan off the heat and stir through the rest of the ingredients, except the ricotta and egg. Leave to cool.

Next, add the ricotta and egg and beat together into a smooth mixture.

Preheat the oven to 200°C/180°C fan/Gas 6.

Roll out the pastry to the thickness of a pound coin and, using a 10–12cm pastry cutter (or anything similar in the kitchen that will do the job), cut out 10 pastry discs.

Place a tablespoon of the filling onto each disc before wetting the sides and closing, making sure you have sealed the parcels well with no air bubbles.

Brush with the egg glaze and bake for 20 minutes until golden brown. Leave to cool slightly before dusting with icing sugar.

Try them for breakfast like they do in Naples, with a strong espresso.

The word 'cannoli' is actually the plural for the singular 'cannolo', but once you have tried one, it is instantly clear why the plural is the word that has stuck. Originating from Sicily, cannoli are small tubes of fried dough filled with sweet ricotta and we became slightly addicted to them during our pilgrimage. We can safely say they played a large part in us putting on a combined 3 stone in weight over 6 weeks.

CANNOLI WITH MOSCATO

MAKES 12 CANNOLI

SICILY

For the filling
600g ricotta cheese
150g icing sugar
Vanilla pod, split lengthways
    and seeds scraped out (or
    1 teaspoon vanilla extract)
Good pinch of cinnamon
    and nutmeg
Small handful of chocolate
    chips and candied fruit
    (optional)

For the shells
250g plain flour
1 egg
1 teaspoon cocoa powder
60ml moscato
25g caster sugar
30g softened butter
Groundnut or vegetable oil,
    for deep-frying

Grated dark chocolate,
    to decorate
Icing sugar, to decorate
Sicilian moscato dessert
    wine, to serve

First, make the filling by beating all of the filling ingredients together in a bowl. The sugar should dissolve into the ricotta, making a smooth, shiny mixture. Spoon into a freezer bag, seal and put in the fridge to rest.

To make the shells, beat together all of the ingredients using a bowl and wooden spoon or by pulsing them together in a food processor.

Once the dough has come together, cover with cling film and rest in the fridge for 30 minutes.

Once rested, roll out your dough to a 4mm thickness and cut out 12 squares, about the same size as a Post-it note.

Now – there's a bit of DIY here – you need something to wrap your shells around. We've found the easiest thing to do is to buy some wooden dowel (the same width as a broom handle) from the hardware shop and get them to cut it to 15cm lengths. You can buy proper cannoli moulds, but it's really not necessary.

Take each dough square and wrap it round a dowel so that the opposite corners meet and seal to make the shell. Twist each shell off the dowel.

Heat the oil to 180°C (if a cube of bread browns in 15–20 seconds, the oil is hot enough). Taking care of the hot oil, deep-fry the cannoli in batches for 2–3 minutes until golden brown and crisp. Remove from the oil and drain on kitchen paper.

Cut the corner off the end of the freezer bag to make an improvised piping bag and fill the shells at each end, working from the middle to make sure they're completely filled.

Dust with grated dark chocolate and icing sugar and serve with Sicilian moscato wine.

These truffles are our homage to a certain famous Italian chocolate, much loved by ambassadors that spoil their guests (...ahem). We've laced ours with Frangelico, a northern Italian liqueur and the hazelnut cousin of the more popular almond-based amaretto. No booze cabinet is complete without it, mostly because the bottle is shaped to look like a monk, complete with a white knotted cord around the waist. Also, the Frangelico Martini (Google it, you can thank us later).

OUR FRANGELICO–LACED HAZELNUT TRUFFLES

MAKES 30 TRUFFLES

PIEDMONT

125ml double cream
50g caster sugar
125g dark chocolate
40ml Frangelico liqueur
200g whole hazelnuts

First, make the ganache by heating the cream and sugar together in a saucepan until the sugar has melted but the cream hasn't boiled.

Break up the chocolate into a mixing bowl and pour over the hot cream. Stir until the chocolate has melted. Add the Frangelico liqueur.

Cover the bowl with cling film and place in the fridge until the ganache has set.

Preheat the oven to 200°C/180°C fan/Gas 6.

Toast the hazelnuts in the oven for about 5 minutes until they have turned golden brown. If the hazelnuts still have their skins on, rub with a tea towel and the skins should come off easily.

Save 30 whole hazelnuts and crush the rest by putting them in a tea towel and hitting them with anything heavy you can get your hands on (rolling pin vs saucepan – it's up to you).

Take the bowl from the fridge and use a teaspoon to dig out nuggets of the ganache.

Push a whole hazelnut into the middle of each nugget and roll into a ball before rolling in the crushed hazelnuts.

The ONLY way to serve these is to stack them into a pyramid, impractically high on a tray, and insist that everyone calls you 'Ambassador'.

Cantuccini are more of a sweet snack than a pudding. These moreish little biscotti from Tuscany are the kind of thing that would accompany the double espressos we drank while piloting our little Ape. We were driving (and driving, and driving), which meant we had to stick to the coffee and avoid the Vin Santo. If you are not driving, we recommend that you don't.

Cantuccini with Vin Santo

TUSCANY

MAKES 40–50 CANTUCCINI

300g plain flour
300g caster sugar
300g whole almonds
  (skin on)
1 teaspoon baking powder
Pinch of ground cinnamon
Pinch of sea salt
3 eggs
2 teaspoons vanilla extract
Egg glaze made from 1 egg
  and 1 egg yolk, beaten
  together

Preheat the oven to 180°C/160°C fan/Gas 4.

In a bowl, mix together all of the ingredients except those for the egg glaze, until a smooth dough is formed.

Cut the dough in two and roll out two 30cm loaves.

Place the loaves on a flat baking sheet lined with parchment paper and, using your fingertips, lightly flatten the loaves.

Brush the loaves generously with the egg glaze. Bake in the oven for around 20 minutes until the loaves are firm and have taken on a shiny golden colour.

Take the loaves out of the oven and cut them diagonally into slices around 1.5cm thick.

Arrange the slices, cut side facing up, on the parchment paper and bake for a further 10–15 minutes at the same temperature until the cantuccini are crisp and golden.

They're great warm from the oven, but they will also keep in an airtight container for at least a week.

Amaretti, the small almond-flavoured biscuits, are the perfect accompaniment to chocolate and they bring an instantly recognizable flavour to these baked puddings. You can buy them in all good Italian delis. Make sure you get the ones wrapped in tissue paper – you can keep children (and adults) amused for hours by setting light to the wrappers and watching them disappear in a puff of smoke. You'll end up throwing away the biscuits just to see the wrapper trick again! But back to the issue in hand – a delicious chocolate pudding...

CHOCOLATE AND AMARETTI PUDDINGS

MAKES 4 PUDDINGS

LOMBARDY

100ml milk
100ml double cream
50g butter
200g dark chocolate, broken up into pieces
2 egg yolks
100g icing sugar, sieved
150g amaretti biscuits, plus extra to serve
100ml amaretto liqueur, plus extra to serve

In a medium saucepan, heat the milk, cream and butter until just before it boils.

Take off the heat and stir in the chocolate until it has completely melted. Leave to cool for about 10 minutes.

Once cooled, beat in the egg yolks and icing sugar.

Break up the amaretti biscuits into your serving glasses and pour a trickle of amaretto into each glass.

Spoon in the chocolate mixture, halfway up the glass, before repeating the process with another biscuit/liqueur layer and chocolate to the top.

Leave to set in the fridge for at least a couple of hours or, even better, leave it overnight.

Serve with more amaretti biscuits and an ice-cold glass of amaretto.

You owe it to your younger, school-dinner-eating self to give rice pudding a go. Trying this Tuscan classic after a long day of Ape driving (which is tiring work, we can assure you), we were completely converted. It is one of the most warming, life-affirming dishes you could possibly hope for.

Italian rice pudding

TUSCANY

SERVES 4

1 tablespoon butter
100g Arborio rice
500ml whole milk
Vanilla pod, split lengthways
   with the seeds scraped out
50g caster sugar, plus extra
   for the topping
2 egg yolks
Pinch of ground nutmeg

This is like making a risotto really, using the same rice and stirring constantly to coax out the rice starch and achieve a rich texture.

Melt the butter in a pan and add the rice, toasting the rice in the butter like you do with a risotto.

Stir in the milk, vanilla seeds and pod and the sugar and slowly cook for around 20 minutes, stirring regularly, until the rice is tender.

Take off the heat and stir in the egg yolks and nutmeg.

You can eat it straight away (like a sweet risotto) or pour the rice into a shallow gratin dish and lightly dust with caster sugar.

Use a blowtorch or a hot grill to caramelize the sugar, forming a crust.

Semifreddo, as the name suggests, is 'semi-cold' and not quite an ice cream. It's a great one to try at home as there's no custard to make and you don't need an ice-cream churner. All the air is whisked into the mix before it's frozen, meaning you end up with a creamy but light texture. The limoncello and raspberries in our version cut through the cream, keeping it light, but equally you can make chocolate or honey versions that pack a richer punch.

LIMONCELLO SEMIFREDDO WITH FRESH RASPBERRIES

SERVES 4

CAMPANIA

4 large eggs
100g caster sugar, plus
   1 tablespoon for
   the compote
Grated zest and juice
   of 1 lemon
Pinch of sea salt
500ml double cream
150ml Limoncello (see our
   recipe on page 193)
Couple of good handfuls
   of raspberries

This recipe starts with a whisk and lots of bowls, just to warn you...

Separate the egg whites and yolks into two mixing bowls. Add the sugar and the lemon zest to the yolks and whisk until pale and smooth. Whisk the egg whites with the pinch of salt until you get stiff peaks.

In a third bowl, whip the cream to soft peaks.

Fold together the cream, egg yolk mixture and limoncello before gently folding in the egg whites and one handful of the raspberries. You should be left with a light, mousse-like mixture studded with the raspberries.

Pour into a cling-filmed loaf tin, add more cling film on top and freeze until needed – at least 6 hours.

Using your hands, squash together the rest of the raspberries with the lemon juice and the extra tablespoon of sugar. This will come together into a fresh raspberry compote.

To serve, take the semifreddo from the freezer and leave in the fridge for 10–15 minutes to warm up slightly.

Remove from the loaf tin and take off the cling film. Cut a thick slice and serve with the raspberry compote and maybe a shot of ice-cold limoncello as well.

Coffee is not a laughing matter in Italy. You will, undoubtedly, get a better coffee in an Italian petrol station than you might find in a Michelin-starred restaurant in England. Another thing that the Italians know a thing or two about is gelato. And olive oil – they are keen on that, too. And balsamic vinegar. We Brits can, however, stake a strong claim to knowing a thing or two about strawberries. Phew! We serve these ice-cream combos at our rooftop pop-up pizzeria, Forza Win, in the summer – simple yet real show stoppers.

Coffee and three ways with vanilla gelato
ACROSS ITALY

Affogato – classic Italian gelato 'drowned' in espresso

Pour freshly made, hot espresso over vanilla ice cream and eat immediately. That's it! But as the coffee begins to melt the ice cream, you'll understand why Italians love this dish so much...

Extra virgin olive oil and sea salt

Even simpler than affogato. Take a ball of good-quality vanilla ice cream and season with a trickle of the best-quality olive oil you can find and a small pinch of good sea salt. The sweetness of the ice cream brings out the fruity and grassy flavours in the oil that are often missed when using it in savoury dishes. The salt balances the sweetness and also brings out the flavour in the oil. This was a huge favourite at our supper club, Forza Win.

Strawberries and balsamic vinegar

Hull (take off the green bits) and quarter a large handful of strawberries and place in a bowl with a tablespoon of sugar and 40ml balsamic vinegar. Stir well and leave to macerate for a couple of hours in the fridge. The vinegar and sugar will bring out the juices from the strawberries and create the most intensely strawberry-flavoured liquor. It's fantastic served with vanilla ice cream.

Panna cotta is a shining example of Italian pudding names that sound glamorous, but have very literal translations, in this case 'cooked cream'. Panna cotta is the Italian take on the nursery classic 'blancmange', save the fancy mould. Our version, flavoured with vanilla and served with honey and toasted pine nuts, is a perfect marriage of flavours and a great way to end a big meal.

Panna cotta with honey and toasted pine nuts

MAKES 4 PANNA COTTAS

PIEDMONT

300ml double cream
100ml whole milk
100g caster sugar
Vanilla pod, split lengthways
    with the seeds scraped out
2 leaves of gelatin
2 tablespoons good honey
Big handful of pine nuts,
    lightly toasted in a dry
    frying pan or under the grill

In a saucepan, heat the cream, milk, sugar and vanilla pod and seeds, taking the pan off the heat before it boils.

Soak the gelatin in cold water until it softens, squeeze away any excess water in your hand and then whisk it into the hot cream and milk mixture.

Divide the mixture among four ramekins that have been brushed with oil. Place in the fridge overnight to set the gelatin.

To turn out, dip the ramekins in boiling water, making sure you get no water in them. This should slightly melt the edges meaning you can invert each ramekin onto a plate and the panna cotta will slide out.

Serve with a trickle of good honey and some toasted pine nuts scattered on top.

This is the first example, and probably the last, of the Italians acknowledging that the English have created something passable in the kitchen. The recipe calls for a strange, bright red liqueur called alchermes. Not to put you off, but this ancient Florentine drink gets its colour from a parasitic insect called a kermes (mmmmmm). We didn't know this when we tried it in Parma, but it's testament to the fact that anything served with custard works!

ZUPPA INGLESE
('ENGLISH SOUP' — THE ITALIAN VERSION OF ENGLISH TRIFLE)

SERVES 4—6

EMILIA-ROMAGNA

For the custard
800ml milk
Grated zest of 1 lemon
7 egg yolks
200g caster sugar
200g plain flour
50g cocoa powder
50g dark chocolate, broken
  up into pieces

For the syrup
50g sugar
150ml alchermes
25 savoiardi biscuits or
  ladyfingers
Whipped cream and
  hundreds and thousands,
  to decorate

To make the custard, bring the milk and lemon zest to the boil in a saucepan. Once boiling, take off the heat and leave to infuse for 10 minutes. Fish out the lemon zest.

In a mixing bowl, whisk together the egg yolks, sugar and flour until smooth and pale. Pour the hot milk over the egg mixture and whisk vigorously until it has combined. Return the mixture to the pan and cook on a low heat, stirring constantly, until the mixture has thickened, coating the back of a spoon.

Pour half of the custard into a bowl, cover with cling film and leave to cool in the fridge. Add the cocoa powder and chocolate to the other half of the custard and stir until the chocolate has melted. Pour into a bowl, cover with cling film and cool in the fridge.

To make the alchermes syrup, heat the sugar and 50ml water until the sugar has dissolved. Boil for a couple of minutes, then add the alchermes and leave to cool.

Find a large glass bowl (preferably a trifle bowl). Dunk the savoiardi biscuits in the alchermes syrup and form a layer in the bottom of the bowl. Spoon in a layer of the custard before another layer of the soaked biscuits, followed by a layer of the chocolate custard. Repeat this process until you have used up all the ingredients.

In the spirit of a trifle, finish with whipped cream and the tackiest hundreds and thousands you can find…

DIY Limoncello

CAMPANIA

For most British people – well, for us anyway – limoncello is the drink you never order. It just arrives, as if by magic, after you finish your meal in that small beachside Italian restaurant on your summer holiday. And the fact that it is doled out for free means (we're assuming) that this limoncello, the one you never ordered, is probably not the finest quality.

We were lucky enough to experience the real deal, spending a day at the Limoncello di Capri production plant on the island of Capri. It turns out that proper limoncello is a complete revelation – bursting with lemony flavour. And, because it's just flavoured alcohol and not distilled, it's easy to make it at home (as long as you're good at zesting lemons and waiting!). You will not regret it and you can give it away for free when you've next got friends round for dinner. Alternatively, give them the bill (service included). It's up to you!

8 unwaxed lemons
70cl bottle of vodka (40% alcohol) (as good as you can afford, but don't go mad, we like Chase Vodka)
500g caster sugar

Using a vegetable peeler, peel the zests off the lemons, making sure not to have any of the bitter white pith attached.

Steep the zest in the bottle of vodka in an airtight container for 10 days at room temperature.

In a saucepan, heat the sugar and 300ml water until the sugar has visibly disappeared, then boil for a couple of minutes, leave to cool and you have a thick sugar syrup.

Stir into the vodka and leave to stand, with the lid on, overnight at room temperature.

Strain through a clean tea towel and bottle into two 500ml sterilized presentation bottles (just immerse them in boiling water) or a wine bottle and just drink the extra limoncello! Chill in the freezer for at least an hour before drinking.

THE NEGRONI

TUSCANY

It took us 25 years to like Campari. Our dad used to drink it all the time and we remember thinking that nothing on earth could ever be so disgusting. Now, finally, we can see what he was on about. Made from a blend of herbs and fruits (a secret recipe no doubt) it is bitter, sweet and aromatic all at the same time. Plus, it is allegedly good for you! It can be drunk neat (for the super brave) or mixed with soda or orange juice. The Negroni, however, is the ultimate way to savour Campari. Negroni is a strong, gin-based aperitif and as Orson Welles once said, 'The bitters are excellent for your liver, the gin is bad for you. They balance each other.' Well said.

1 part London dry gin (we like Tanqueray)
1 part Campari
1 part vermouth (ideally something better than Martini, but that will do!)
Orange twist, to garnish

Mix the ingredients with cracked ice and stir until very cold. Serve in a manly glass (something you could imagine Don Draper with, ideally) over ice cubes. Garnish with a twist of orange.

BELLINI

VENETO

Synonymous with Venice, the Bellini was invented in Harry's Bar behind Saint Mark's Square in the 1930s. It is named after the famous Venetian painter from the fifteenth century because of its pink colour (apparently he liked to paint with pink). I can honestly say if you ever find yourself in Venice, do NOT bother with Harry's Bar – it is overpriced and looks like the inside of the Rovers Return. Do make sure you have a Bellini, though – just have it somewhere else.

2 white peaches, stones removed
Prosecco

Pulp your peaches in a blender or food processor and then pass through a sieve.

Divide your peach mixture between two champagne glasses. Top up the glasses with Prosecco (about one part peach to two parts Prosecco). Drink. Easy.

The Spritz

MAKES 1 COCKTAIL

VENETO

Aperol is a kind of baby brother to Campari – less bitter, half the amount of alcohol, generally more approachable. There is only one way to drink Aperol and that is as a Spritz. This is probably the perfect summer drink, but as you can see from these photos, it also works well at a party in December.

3 parts Prosecco or Italian white wine
2 parts Aperol or 2 parts Campari (for the real men)
1 part soda water
Orange slice and the plumpest green olive you can get your hands on (with the stone in), to garnish

The Spritz presents you with a few options: Prosecco vs wine and Aperol vs Campari. We suggest you try them all and find out which is your favourite.

To make a Spritz, pour the Prosecco/wine over ice cubes. Then add the Aperol/Campari and top up with the soda water. Add a slice of orange and the olive pierced with a large cocktail stick. Venice in a glass.

ITALIAN INGREDIENTS BUYING GUIDE

Some of the dishes in this book use produce that are somewhat specialist. This is our guide to where to find them.

Online:

One of the best ways to find more obscure ingredients is to look online. You can now get home delivery nationwide and often at a fraction of the cost of high street delis. Here are our favourites:

www.nifeislife.com A great place for cheese and meats. Some of the best Buffalo mozzarella we've tried outside of Italy and everything from mortadella to tubs of pork lard (good for our Piadina recipe).

www.natoora.co.uk A wonderful site for fresh fruit, veg and herbs. Everything from whole globe artichokes to fresh oregano. Incredible citrus fruit section with everything from Sicilian blood oranges, Amalfi lemons and Calabrian bergamots.

www.wearethesauce.com A great new setup dedicated to bringing you the freshest produce directly from Italy without the middle man.

www.dingley-dell.com The man to go to for wood-fired ovens, his passion knows no bounds.

www.fornobravoukshop.co.uk Forno Bravo is the UK's leading site for wood-fired pizza ovens and amateur pizza chefs with great tutorials and forums to read. They have a wide selection of pizza equipment and sell Caputo '00' flour in 1kg bags.

www.certainlywood.co.uk The place to buy kiln dried logs and kindling in bulk, for the wood-fired oven enthusiast.

Our locals in Soho, London:

Berwick Street Market – Berwick St.
All of our fruit, veg and herbs come from the guys on the market. They have an amazing selection of seasonal produce at a fraction of the price of the supermarket!

i Camisa & Son – 61 Old Compton St.
A fantastic traditional Italian deli right in the heart of Soho. This family run place is a shrine to all things Italian.

Gelupo gelato – 7 Archer St.
True Italian gelato that is so good we still eat it in January. They supplied the ice cream for Forza Win and if it is sunny their granitas can't be missed.

Lina Stores – 18 Brewer St.
A beautiful shop that sells the finer things of Italian life. Their fresh pasta is second to none.

Bar Italia – 22 Frith St.
A little slice of Italy in Soho, and the punchiest Espresso this side of Naples.

Polpo – 41 Beak St.
A Venetian baccaro (of sorts) with the best polpette and Aperol spritz in town.

INDEX

ACKNOWLEDGEMENTS

Grazie Mille to:

Our mother for having faith in our decision to stake our future in a three wheeled oven/van (or at least pretending to) and to our father who would have loved all this.

Jemma for agreeing to marry Thom during the most hectic year ever – and putting up with all the late nights and antisocial hours (as well as getting stuck in whatever the hangover).

Louis for being the 3rd pilgrim, 'dough baller extraordinaire' and for sticking with us during a memorable first year. We couldn't have done it without you.

Antonino and Stefano, our Neapolitan pizza gurus, for showing us how it's done.

Oscar, Johnny H, Johnny C, Johnny Steen, Jack, George, Yasemin, Rosie, Mai, Ed J, Charlotte, Chris, Zanny, Clemmie, Joe, Razvan, Steven, Gabby, Anthony, Bruno, Tom, Koj, Alison, Holly, Eloise, Sarah, Will, Craig and Pascale for helping us take our little van to markets, parties, festivals and the International Vertical Dance Championships whilst keeping it all such fun!

Petra, Ian, Millie, Bowler Jez, Bangra Alec, Jamon Nick, Wild Andy, Ru & Annie, Free Bird James, Bahn Mi Ha, Bread Man Chris, Falafel Omar, The Rib Man, Rainbo Ben and Shrimp, Tongue 'n' Cheek Christiano and Patty & Bun Joe for making the London street food scene what it is.

Bash Redford for his endless enthusiasm and for creating our rooftop pizzeria 'Forza Win' with us. Also to Terry for 'smoking it' up and down the M4 and helping us bring Terrina to life. Let's never build another one tonne pizza oven on the roof of a five story building with no lift though.

Terry, Alex, Jimmy, Norman, Matt, Garry, Ross and the rest of the Berwick street fruit and veg boys who have been a font of 'market nous' and bad jokes over the past year.

Billy, Kerry, Darren, Ed and Cindy for giving us a roof over our head.

Simon for supplying the booze.

Ben and Carlos at Rampage Studios along with Steven, Rob, Rolo, Amanda, and Brave Gianluca for bringing the pilgrimage to life and for playing as hard as we worked.

The team at HarperCollins: Carole for saying yes. Helen for keeping everything on track and putting up with last-minute changes. Martin and Lucy for making it look so fantastic. To Myles, Alice, Maddie, Tony and Tom for the beautiful photos and making the shoots such fun. To Erin, Laura, Orlando, Claire, James and Carly for their enthusiasm and for making this whole process such a pleasure.

And finally brilliant, mad, funny, and determined Diana, who saw an article in a local paper about two muppets driving back from Italy in a ridiculous van and thinking 'There's a book in that'.

HarperCollins*Publishers*
77–85 Fulham Palace Road,
Hammersmith, London W6 8JB

www.harpercollins.co.uk

First published by HarperCollins*Publishers* 2013

1 3 5 7 9 10 8 6 4 2

A catalogue record of this book is available from
the British Library

ISBN 978-0-00-750430-5

Food stylist: Alice Hart
Props stylist: Tony Hutchinson

Printed and bound in Italy by L.E.G.O. S.p.A.